Catholic Schools

Colin Brooksbank

What an uplifting read for a life-long educator! The writer has given a very fresh and faith filled way to reflect upon teaching as a vocation, particularly in Catholic education. It provides a rich resource for reflecting on our practice and lives. It is a very optimistic book and awakens the spirit of gratefulness and privilege in being part of the teaching profession. The book will have many uses for both new and experienced educators, administrators and governors for reflection, formation, and re-energising. I look forward to seeing the publication of this refreshing book. It certainly has a place in enhancing Catholic education at a time when we are attempting to communicate our role and distinctiveness in a rapidly changing context.

Dr Marie Emmitt
Executive Dean
Faculty of Education
Australian Catholic University

A treasure trove of reflections, quotations, anecdotes and prayers... so much inspiration. Here is a series of sayings that speak to the ministry of teaching in profound and reflective ways.

Dr William Sultmann AM
Associate Professor and Deputy Dean
La Salle Academy
Australian Catholic University

Colin Brooksbank has drawn on his long experience as a Catholic educator and his extensive knowledge of scripture, history and literature to write this book of reflections. He has arranged the reflections under a dozen key themes to produce short inspirational, at times challenging, reflections suitable for those ministering in Catholic education. Each bite size reflection will enrich your understanding of the mission of Catholic education. This is a book to be read slowly and thoughtfully.

David J Hutton OAM
Executive Director Emeritus of Catholic Education
Archdiocese of Brisbane

Saint Ignatius realised back in the sixteenth century that the imagination provided a pathway to faith that was just as significant as doctrine or deduction. More recent scholars have also emphasised the power of story and poetry as evocative avenues into vocation and meaning. *Catholic Schools* provides an evocative treasure trove of quotes for anyone seeking inspiration about the deeper purposes and aspirations of Catholic education.

Dr Paul Sharkey
Postgraduate Coordinator
Catholic Theological College
Melbourne

Experience
Achievement, Encouragement
Challenge

Catholic Schools

Colin Brooksbank

Published in Australia by
Coventry Press
33 Scoresby Road
Bayswater VIC 3153

ISBN 9781922589606

Copyright © Colin Brooksbank 2024

All rights reserved. Other than for the purposes and subject to the conditions prescribed under the *Copyright Act*, no part of this publication may be reproduced, stored in a retrieval system, or transmitted in any form or by any means, electronic, mechanical, photocopying, recording or otherwise, without the prior permission of the publisher.

Old Testament Scripture quotations are from Ronald Knox, *The Holy Bible: A Translation From the Latin Vulgate in the Light of the Hebrew and Greek Originals*. London: Burns and Oates, 1948.
New Testament Scripture quotations are from James A. Kleist SJ and Joseph Lilly CM, *The New Testament*, Milwaukee: The Bruce Publishing Company, 1956.

Nihil Obstat:	Rev. Dr Cameron Forbes STD
	Diocesan Censor
Imprimatur:	Very Reverend Anthony Kerin JCL VG
	Vicar General
	Archdiocese of Melbourne
Date:	19 August 2024

The Nihil Obstat and Imprimatur are official declarations that a book or pamphlet is free of doctrinal or moral error. No implication is contained therein that those who have granted the Nihil Obstat and Imprimatur agree with the contents, opinions or statements expressed. They do not necessarily signify that the work is approved as a basic text for catechetical instruction.

Catalogue-in-Publication entry is available from the National Library of Australia
http://catalogue.nla.gov.au

Cover design by Ian James – www.jgd.com.au
Text design by Coventry Press
Set in EB Garamond
Printed in Australia

... we will not boast beyond our measure but within the measure of the sphere which God apportioned to us...

2 Corinthians 10:13

Contents

Introduction	1
Reflections	7
1. A proud profession	9
2. On faith: a yardstick	10
3. On being called: the place where we belong	39
4. On dedication: being there for the long haul	53
5. On co-operation: working in association with our colleagues	63
6. On mindfulness: being centred	78
7. On teaching: teaching and learning	91
8. On care: the work of mind and heart	138
9. On witness: delivering the message by word and deed	153
10. On cultural awareness: reading the signs of the times	164
11. On a humane approach: a wise vision of the human condition	191
12. On balance: 'sanctified common sense'	208
13. On weighing it all up: achievements	220
Some prayers for teachers	225

Introduction

A banner in an election campaign proclaimed, 'If you can read this, thank a teacher'.

Even in our darker moments, we have to acknowledge that we as teachers have achieved much – not as much as we would have liked – but much all the same.

Aspects of our achievements are considered in the reflections that follow.

Much of our adult life is spent in earning a living, To a greater or lesser extent, the way we earn our living shapes our lives: as teachers, most obviously in our daily schedules and the structure of our year. Moreover, people's professions colour their way of thinking and their priorities in the interpretation of many of life's circumstances. And thus it is with teachers: our calling involves a distinctive outlook and associated activities and duties

When we were undertaking our preparation to be teachers, we would have undertaken a unit or units like 'The Philosophy of Education' or 'The Foundations of Education'. Sadly, it's quite possible that in our anxiety to survive in the classroom, we considered these units to be superfluous to our needs.

Now that we are in the thick of our professional lives, as we regularly reflect on the practice of our craft, we may also at times wonder where our efforts figure in the grand scheme of things.

As teachers in a Catholic school, we may also wonder about the claims its ethos might have on us.

The reflections offered in the following pages are designed to address such issues through considering how our professional ideals may find expression in the practicalities of the classroom.

Introduction

Further, teaching in a Catholic school is recognised as a ministry: the bishop of their diocese delegates to teachers the transmission of Catholic doctrines, traditions and practices. If this sounds somewhat lofty, we are quickly grounded by the reality of our daily interaction with groups of students, colleagues and parents.

This interaction is the distinctive way we love God and our neighbour. (The same can be said for neurosurgeons, nurses, plumbers, janitors... and for every other calling – each has its own manner of loving God and others.)

Given today's circumstances, it is possible that the school is the only point of contact between some children and the Church. It is also probable that in our school there will be children and colleagues, members of another, or no, denomination, who have nevertheless chosen to be associated with a Catholic school.

Such are some contexts of our interactions.

There is another context of which some teachers, parents, colleagues and students may be unaware.

An analogy may help. We are conscious of the buildings in which we teach, but few, if any of us think about the foundations on which they are built.

The Catholic schools of today are built upon the work of thousands of Sisters, Brothers and Priests. Beginning with the first Catholic popular school in Europe just before 1600, hundreds of Religious Orders were founded with the intention of helping 'the poor, the sick, and the ignorant' as Catherine McAuley described her Sisters' mission. Marcellin Champagnat added the hope that his schools would produce 'good Christians and good people'. Further, John Baptist de la Salle noted that 'the child who knows how to read and write will be capable of anything'.

The beliefs and hopes of these revered founders of Religious orders have become part of our consciousness.

The Founders had a wider vision: having perceived people in need – slaves to be ransomed, or ignorant children faced with limited prospects, for example – they believed that God was calling them to address the issue and that vowed Religious would provide the most effective help.

The Founders' vision was often formed over time, through experience, and in accordance with practices current in the Church. Thus, in collaboration with their early followers, they selected a Habit, their daily routine, a Religious Rule, and devotions and practices that expressed their unique charism.

Teaching orders flourished particularly in the nineteenth century and the first half of the twentieth. Since then, there has been a very rapid decline in their numbers, so that the presence of a Religious in schools is something of a rarity. Coupled with the loss of numbers is the progressive revelation of numerous cases of abuse in Catholic educational institutions. The labours and sacrifices of so many good Religious women and men – the majority – are unfortunately in danger of being forgotten.

While lay people who have succeeded Religious cannot be expected to adopt their regimen, the spirit that animated them and the strategies they employed are legacies that teachers in Catholic schools are challenged to aspire to and adopt.

This is not to imply that lay people are meant to be religious in disguise. The laity lead their lives in their families and society with their own set of ideals and demands.

The ideals proposed here *are* ideals: attitudes and codes of behaviour which we are invited to work towards adopting. People who do not share the religious background to the ideals are invited to understand and respect them

In practice our inherited ideals and strategies may be expressed in the following way. (Underlined terms are considered in the reflections that follow.)

Introduction

<u>Faith</u> tells us that we are <u>called</u> to be teachers, not working alone, but in <u>co-operation</u> with our colleagues. Faith is the source of <u>dedication</u> to our calling. Influenced by our faith and dedication, our professional life is characterised by <u>mindfulness</u>, <u>teaching</u>, <u>care</u>, <u>guidance</u>, <u>witness</u>, <u>cultural awareness</u>, <u>a humane approach</u> and <u>balance</u>.

Teachers who read the reflections may wish to consider some points prayerfully

That practical man, St Thomas More, is one of many to whom the following prayer has been attributed: 'The things I pray for, Lord, give me the strength to strive for'. (We may feel it is more a case of 'The things I strive for, give me the strength to pray for'.)

That equally practical woman, St Teresa of Avila, had much the same to say:

The best effects [of prayer] are those followed by actions, so that we do not merely desire the honour of God but really work for it.

***

A word about scriptural quotations: a few are taken from the Douay Version: most of those from the Old Testament are taken from the translation by Monsignor Ronald Knox; most Gospel references are from the translation by Fr James A Kleist SJ, while most references from the other New Testament books are from the translation by Fr Joseph L Lilly CM. These translations will not be familiar to most readers, and may thus help to impart a certain freshness to well-known scriptural texts.

***

A word about where the reflections come from: basically, from the experiences of a teacher who spent a lifetime in Catholic education.

After an Archbishop made a polite inquiry about his plans, a young teacher replied that he was going to teach in a Catholic school. When the Archbishop commented: 'Make sure you do something apostolic – join the St Vincent de Paul Society', the person was surprised because he had assumed that teaching in a Catholic school had something to do with being apostolic. That was in the days when Sisters, Brothers and Priests formed the majority of teachers in Catholic schools. Through their Rule and their three-hundred-and-fifty-year history, Religious, aware of the spiritual foundation of their work, approached it with confidence and enthusiasm.

In a relatively short period, the teacher witnessed lay teachers making up the majority of staff. At the same time, the Religious training colleges, opened first to lay women and then males, became Colleges of Advanced Education, and like the schools, received government funding (it survived a challenge in the High Court). Schools became co-educational, lay people became Department Heads, then Principals, and finally Diocesan Directors of Catholic Education.

The transitions caused much pain to Religious who felt the severance of their ties with institutions and projects of which they were justly proud. It took time for lay people to be considered capable – not to mention worthy – of fulfilling the roles that were handed to them by default. Lay people continue to reflect on their roles.

All teachers have been affected by seemingly endless curricular reforms and modifications, not to mention disputes over pay and expectations about teachers' lifestyle. Confidence has been challenged by scandals revealed through inquiries.

Over the years and witnessing these events as a participant, the teacher discussed them and related issues with Sisters, Brothers and Priests, theologians, academics in Australia and overseas and with colleagues in the day-to-day life of the staffroom. He also did

Introduction

research in the extensive documentation that has been produced since the late 60s.

Therefore, were the Archbishop to pose his question today, the teacher's discussions, research and experience would enable him to declare confidently that teaching in a Catholic school can be an apostolic activity, and, moreover, he could confidently assert there are inherited principles to guide teachers who wish to engage in it.

Hence the reflections.

Reflections

1

A proud profession

As we begin our reflections, we have every reason to be optimistic

We belong to a proud profession, the midwife of all other callings.

We have our own successes and we witness the achievements of our colleagues and the successes of our school.

We acknowledge that we live in an imperfect world, and recognise that individually and collectively we have at times fallen short of the mark.

All the same, we have our ideals; individually and collectively we try to live up to them.

And when we get a little better, when our students get a little better, the world itself is that much a little better.

2

On faith: a yardstick

> But since we have the same spirit of faith as shown in the Scripture passage 'I believe therefore I spoke', we also believe and that is why we also speak.
>
> 2 Corinthians 4:13

The term 'spirit of faith' implies not only acts of belief but also a persistent, guiding outlook – a moral compass, as it were.

All Christians are invited to be guided by faith as they go about the duties of their calling.

And so it is with teachers who speak because they believe.

Faith is needed to view the whole enterprise of our school as an instrument of God's work in the world.

Sometimes, a deep faith is needed when teachers, confronted by certain children, recall Jesus' words: 'Whoever receives one of these little children receives me' (Mark 9:37).

Sometimes, a deep faith is needed when we have dealings with difficult colleagues or parents.

Sometimes, a deep faith is needed when we are faced with a succession of bureaucratic mandates and unreasonable demands.

At times, a deep faith is needed to make sense of humdrum duties.

(Of course, it would be fanciful to maintain that teaching is the only profession to suffer from the humdrum: even the most prestigious occupations have their tedious hours.)

Faith

> He didn't rate God very highly.

In Walker Percy's novel, *The Adventures of a Bad Catholic at a Time near the End of the World*, Dr Thomas More states that, while he is a believer, he rates love for God behind love of women, whiskey and music in that order; moreover, as for his fellow man, he didn't love him at all...

Dr More (imagined to be a descendant of St Thomas More) lives in a dystopian world and a dystopian Church: through More's adventures and associations, the author has much to say about practices and tendencies in the Catholic Church.

Doctor More judges himself with disarming honesty.

We may perhaps give thought to our own faith and priorities.

Faith

> 'Oh I believe in God all right, but I hate him because of what he's done to me.'
>
> Sentiments of a recovering alcoholic.

This poor woman was reflecting on her alcoholism and the circumstances that drove her to it.

It is possible that some time in our professional life, we will encounter misfortune. Sometimes, we may bring it on ourselves. At other times, troubles may happen to us without any of our own doing: even the psalmist protested that, although the Israelites had been keeping all the rules, disaster had come upon them (Psalm 138)

Sufferings can be so intense that religious ideas can seem like figments of the imagination.

It's said that St Vincent de Paul put two pins in the shape of a cross inside his soutane: his trials tested his faith so much that touching the cross became his act of faith.

We feel for any members of our school community whose faith is being tested by their sufferings.

Faith

> O the mind, mind has mountains, cliffs of fall
> Frightful, sheer no man fathomed...
>
> Gerard Manley Hopkins (1844-1889), 'No worst there is none...'

These lines are from one of the six poems by Hopkins that are called 'Terrible Sonnets', so named because they describe the mental terrors that some people experience.

Some who have recovered from mental illness say that they have been in hell – their horror intensified by feeling rejected by everyone, including God.

Without a doubt, we will at some time encounter students, colleagues or parents afflicted in this way.

We have compassion, and offer acts of kindness where we can,
We are grateful to have been spared this illness.

Faith

> As Commandant of Auschwitz, I was responsible for carrying out part of the cruel plans of the 'Third Reich' for human destruction... May the Lord God forgive one day what I have done.
>
> Rudolf Hoess (1901-1947) Commandant of Auschwitz Concentration Camp

We believe in a God who is infinitely powerful, loving and merciful. Only he can make sense of the evil for which Rudolf Hoess was responsible.

At his trial, Hoess was careful to point out that he had been directly responsible for the execution of two and a half million people and indirectly for the death of a half million who died of forced labour, starvation and neglect.

He appeared to be totally unaffected by his crimes.

Among those whom he had rounded up was a community of Jesuits. Their Superior, who had been absent on the day of their arrest, sought to rejoin them in the camp. For some reason, Hoess had him ejected.

Just a few days before he was due to be executed, Hoess asked to see a priest. His request was answered by the Superior mentioned above. Hoess went to Confession. The next day, the day of his execution, he received Communion.

The three million who had died were individually infinitely beloved of God. So was Hoess.

Faith is needed to sustain us as we confront evil that seems to defy explanation.

Faith

> *'Jesus*, remember *me*...'
> '...This very day *you* will be with *me*...'
> Luke 23:43

Not 'Master' or 'Rabbi' or 'Son of David' but 'Jesus'.

In agony, in the midst of shouting and ridicule, the criminal we have come to call 'The Good Thief' entered into a one-on-one relationship with Jesus, calling him by name – and Jesus replied, one-on-one.

The Good Thief was not a theologian, a priest or a mystic, but a criminal who admitted that his punishment was what he deserved.

Faith tells us that we, as individuals, are invited to enter into this one-on-one relationship.

Because we are loved, we try to respond in love by following the teachings of Jesus.

Too often, perhaps, schools have made the mistake of emphasising the rules in themselves, rather than as a response to a one-on-one relationship with Jesus.

Faith

> Judas his betrayer, now realised that judgment had gone against [Jesus], and, stricken with remorse, brought back the thirty pieces of silver to the chief priests and elders. 'It was wrong for me', he said, 'to betray an innocent man'.
>
> Matthew 27:3-4
>
> Peter remembered the Lord's prediction – how he had said to him: 'Today before a cock crows, you will disown me three times'. And he went out and wept bitterly.
>
> Luke 22: 61-2

Both apostles had been with Jesus throughout his ministry. They had both heard his teachings and witnessed his miracles. They had both been sent out to preach and heal the sick, and then returned rejoicing.

Judas betrayed Jesus for money, led the armed party to arrest him, and identified him with a kiss.

Peter evidently had a concealed sword at the Last Supper, used it to injure a servant of the High Priest and then denied Jesus three times.

Both men were filled with regret.

Peter rejoined the other apostles, all of whom had also deserted Jesus.

Judas went off alone and hanged himself.

We are confronted with mysteries, but we can say that Peter's love for Jesus, person-to-person, his confidence in him, had once again sustained him.

Our school tries to help students foster their personal relationship with Jesus as the basis for their faith and confidence, even when, like Peter, they fail.

Faith

> 'Oyez! Oyez!'

The Town Crier's summons (more familiar to us as 'Hear ye! Hear ye!') called people to attend to an authoritative message, containing an instruction or tidings of joy or sorrow.

In the early days of Christianity, converts would have been familiar with the Greek word *euangelion* signifying a serious message delivered by an official envoy.

St Paul and others adopted the term *euangelion* to denote the solemn yet glad tiding that God had visited his people in the life, death and resurrection of Jesus Christ.

When the glad tidings, the *euangelion*, were introduced into England, Anglo-Saxon speakers translated the word as 'Godspel' or 'Good Story'.

It is our privilege to share these good tidings in a way that makes sense to our students.

Faith

> Christ is truly risen!
> He is risen indeed!

This exchange of greetings is used by Orthodox Christians, and middle-eastern Catholics on Easter Sunday and following days.

We believe that Christ is truly risen; the Resurrection is central to Christians' mindset, life and worship.

Paul declared to the Philippians 'I know Christ and what his resurrection can do' (3:10).

Throughout Lent, the liturgy of the Church progressively prepares us to celebrate the Resurrection.

Perhaps we can use parts of Lenten liturgical texts to help our students to deepen their faith in Christ and what his resurrection can do.

Faith

> Praise be to you, my Lord, for our sister, bodily death
> From whom no living person can escape
> St Francis, 'Canticle of the Sun'

When he knew death was approaching, Francis no doubt recalled this verse from the Canticle in which he praised creation. He loved the gifts and the Giver.

His faith led him to see death as a gift.

While his deathbed was marked by acts of prayer and penance, he found joy in the presence of his first follower, Brother Bernard, and his long-time benefactor, the widow 'Brother' Jacqueline. Following a vision in a dream, she hastened from Rome to Assisi, bringing with her the almond cakes which were his favourite. Women were not allowed in the Friary, but in admitting her, Francis recognised that charity is the supreme rule. He did his best to show his appreciation by trying to eat a few crumbs of her almond cakes As St James says, 'Mercy triumphs over judgment'.

A deep faith and enlightened love for others: matters to ponder.

Faith

> Firmly I believe and truly
> God is three and God is one...

These opening lines of a hymn by John Henry Newman, priest, cardinal and now a canonised saint, introduce a short statement of belief.

Elsewhere, Newman had published *A Grammar of Assent*, a treatise on how one might arrive at belief. To be honest, very few of us have read it (and perhaps even fewer have understood it).

Nevertheless, we all have our own story of belief. Some of us have always believed, without ever questioning the fact. Others may have abandoned religious belief for a while or permanently. Still others may have come to believe after long inquiry.

The hymn 'Amazing grace' contains the words ... 'the hour I first believed'.

It may well be beneficial to think about the story of our own belief.

Faith

> We acknowledge the Trinity, holy and perfect, to consist of the Father, the Son and the Holy Spirit. In this Trinity, there is no intrusion of any alien element or of anything from outside, nor is the Trinity a blend of creative and created being. It is a wholly creative and energising reality...
> St Athanasius (296-373)

Athanasius, bishop of Alexandria in Egypt for 45 years, was no armchair warrior. In attesting that the Son is of the same substance as the Father, he was exiled five times; he tangled with several Roman emperors; and he was embroiled in controversy with prominent churchmen. He remained steadfast in defending and clarifying the statement of belief formulated at Nicea (modern day Iznik in Turkey) in 325.

For this reason, a statement of belief in and about the Trinity was for many centuries entitled 'The Athanasian Creed'. Most people these days will be unaware of it.

However, while people use the shamrock or a triangle or other symbols or analogies in a bid to come to terms with the Trinity, the phrase 'A wholly creative and energising reality' invites deeper reflection.

Faith

> 'Did you receive the Holy Spirit when you became believers?' 'We have not even heard there is a Holy Spirit.'
>
> Acts of the Apostles 19:2

On his third missionary journey, St Paul came to Ephesus where he discovered a group of followers of John the Baptist. They had been baptised in his name.

The group were then baptised 'in the name of the Lord Jesus' and when Paul laid hands on them, they received the Holy Spirit.

Perhaps, we may feel a little like these disciples of John: the Holy Spirit may not loom large in our consciousness.

Pope Benedict XVI spoke of 'the beauty of being baptised in the Holy Spirit' when a person is made 'a living member of the mystical Body of Christ'.

These are lofty terms, inviting reflection and study.

Perhaps we and our students can benefit from recalling the times we have recognised Jesus as our Lord, and when we have experienced or been prompted to practise charity, peace, patience, kindness, self-control... among the other qualities listed as fruits of the Spirit in Galatians 5:22. We then realise that the Holy Spirit has been active in our lives all along.

Faith

> ... with the heart a person believes...
> Romans 10:10
>
> I have the faith of a Breton peasant and by the time I die I hope to have the faith of a Breton peasant's wife.
> Louis Pasteur (1822-1895)
>
> I am here to say that I am '... the foe of all gods, who are only imaginary figments and all priests, who are quacks and crooks'.
> Jean-Marie Déguignet (1834-1895) Memories of a Breton Peasant.

Two contemporaries: one, a noted scientist; and the other, at times a soldier, farmer, trader, carer for an alcoholic wife, and writer.

They had polar opposite attitudes to faith.

As we try earnestly to believe with the heart, we recognise that in our family and in the circle of colleagues, parents and students, there will almost certainly be those who have given up, perhaps bitterly.

As St Paul reminds us, this is not the time for premature judgments.

Faith

> 'Pious old frauds.'

In this way, the father of the philosopher and activist, Simone de Beauvoir (1908-1986), assessed her Catholic teachers. After a very devout childhood, she came to describe them as 'comical old church hens'.

New legislation in France had revealed that her teachers lacked professional qualifications and were in other respects deficient. The quips may bring a smile but, to be fair, they make light of the dedicated lives and sincere intentions of the teachers of that time.

Among the young people before us today, there may be brilliant students like Simone de Beauvoir who can choose to respect us or to expose our shortcomings. There will certainly be those who are keen to live their faith in word and deed.

There may well be those who are happy to say and do what is asked of them, but without any conviction. And, as Pope Francis remarked, there could well be those who show 'growing detachment from the practice of the faith'.

Through our grasp of the faith and our skill in presenting it on our students' wavelength, we hope to be genuine witnesses – and certainly not pious frauds.

Faith

> You have faith enough to believe that there is one God. Excellent! The devils have faith like that, and it makes them tremble. But can you not see, you quibbler, that faith divorced from deeds is barren?
>
> James 2:19-20.

Bartolomé de las Casas (1484-1566), born shortly before Columbus' first voyage, joined his father in being one of the early settlers in Hispaniola, which comprises what is now the Dominican Republic and Haiti.

Soon after his arrival in 1502, he was granted an estate or *encomienda*; it was worked by members of the Native population. Ordained a priest at some point before 1510, he continued to profit from slave labour; indeed he participated in the bloody subjugation of Cuba.

One day, when preparing his sermon, he suddenly realised slave labour was wrong. He divested himself of his property and began to take up the cause of the Indians, as they were called. Many of the estate owners, including numerous priests and persons of influence, believed that, because the Natives were less than human, their masters were justified in their acts of cruelty and exploitation. Las Casas incurred their wrath. He returned to Spain where he joined the Dominicans, who had also opposed slavery.

For the remainder of his life he became a constant – some would say, aggressive – critic of slavery, his protests even reaching the King

One day, when he was describing to His Majesty and his court the slaughter of seven thousand children, a bishop protested, 'What is that to me and the king?'

The bishop no doubt had faith, but...

Faith

> So what you have learned and recited back you must store away in your intellect and affections, reciting it in bed, pondering it in your walks, not forgetting it while you eat – letting your affection keep watch over it even when your body sleeps.
>
> St Augustine: *Instructions to the newly-baptised.*

St Augustine was referring to the doctrines summarised in the Apostles' Creed, which had served as the basis for the instruction of the newly-baptised.

He is not talking about isolated acts of assent but rather a spirit of faith which accompanies and inspires a person at all times.

This spirit is meant to engage both the mind and the emotions.

We might recall the Apostles' Creed and from time to time prayerfully consider its articles.

We thank God for our own baptism and initiation into the company of believers.

Faith

> I planted, Apollos watered, but it was God who was all the time giving increase.
>
> 1 Corinthians 3:6

Paul here sees his life's work as a collaboration between God and human beings.

He recognises that the power of his message comes from God.

It is our privilege to be involved in the same work as St Paul, even though we feel insignificant in comparison.

As Jesus says in John's Gospel, one person sows and another reaps. Our collaboration with others may mean that we do not see the results of our work, or even know who our collaborators are: the word that we speak today may bear fruit far in the future.

It will be God who gives the increase.

We thank God for the privilege of working with him, and ask for the faith to see our work in this light.

Faith

> But when Philip came and preached to them about God's kingdom and the name of Jesus Christ, they were baptised, men and women.
>
> Acts 8:12.

Philip was one of the seven deacons chosen to help the apostles.

'They' were Samaritans – looked upon as second rate, as we know.

Furthermore, they had lately been enthralled by Simon the magician, whom they considered some kind of angel.

Such was the power of Philip's preaching and miracles that Simon was among those who were baptised.

Peter and John, having been sent to see what was going on, were moved to call down the Holy Spirit on the converts. Seeing the apostles' power, Simon offered money for a share in it.

We cannot boast of Philip's powers of preaching. However, we can be certain that God will help us to do his work, even with difficult audiences and with those who, like Simon, seem to miss the point entirely.

Faith

> From Syria to Rome on land and sea I fight with beasts... being bound to ten leopards, a band of soldiers who, the more you tip them, the more outrageously they behave.
>
> St Ignatius of Antioch, *Letter to the Romans*

During the reign of the Emperor Trajan (98-117 AD), Ignatius, the Bishop of Antioch in northern Syria, was transported by land and sea to Rome, where, according to tradition, he was tried and thrown to beasts. As the above quotation indicates, in day-to-day matters, he evidently had his feet firmly on the ground.

It is believed that Ignatius and his friend Polycarp (Bishop of Smyrna -Izmir in modern Turkey) were disciples of St John the Apostle.

Ignatius wrote a number of important documents. Among them was the Letter to the Magnesians, to whom he gave the advice:

> Take care to do all things in harmony with God and with the Bishop presiding in the place of God.

From the Apostles and Saints Ignatius and Polycarp and down through a long chain of bishops, saints and sinners, we have our present bishops, successors of the Apostles.

When we say the Apostles' Creed, it is well to recall the venerable inherited Tradition which we believe and are called upon to teach.

For us to do so, our present Bishop has approved our Religious Education program and the processes leading to our accreditation.

In this day and age, he probably has his own set of ten leopards to deal with. We owe him our prayerful and loyal support.

Faith

> He then said to his disciples: 'Have them recline in groups of about fifty each'. They did so, and had them all recline. Then he took the five loaves and the two fish into his hands, and, looking up to heaven said grace over them, and broke them into portions which he gave his disciples to serve to the crowd. All ate, and everyone had a plentiful meal. Besides, what was left over from their meal was gathered up, in all twelve baskets of remnants.
>
> Luke 9:14-17

Here we see the disciples working with Jesus. It must have been hard for them to realise that in managing a tired and hungry crowd, in distributing food and collecting the leftovers, they were involved in the enactment of so great a sign.

Faith tells us that, as teachers, we are involved in working with Jesus to make known his saving influence in students' lives.

Faith also tells us that involvement entails not only teaching, but also the humdrum details of managing people and resources.

We need faith to see the wider significance of seemingly unimportant, even boring, chores.

Faith

> By way of answer they said to him [the man born blind]: 'You were wholly born in sin, and you mean to teach us?' And they expelled him.
>
> Jesus was informed that they had expelled him. When he met the man, he said: 'Do you believe in the Son of God?' 'Well, who is he, sir?' the man answered; 'I want to believe in him'. 'You are now looking in his face', replied Jesus; 'yes, it is he who is now speaking to you!' 'I do believe, sir' he said; and he fell on his knees before him.
>
> John 9:34-38.

A lifetime of blindness and begging had made the man born blind feisty; he was something of an embarrassment to his parents – some held the belief that the man's blindness was in fact caused by his parents' sins, and they may well have feared that this was true. Jesus quickly dismissed the idea.

It was a rollercoaster day for the man born blind: he was cured after going through an elaborate ritual; he became a minor celebrity; after interrogation, he was expelled from the synagogue, and, finally, he was led to look into the face of his deliverer.

Jesus looked for the outcast and led him, through his experiences, to make a leap of faith.

Jesus is our model as teachers when we have to deal with feisty students.

Faith

> Let us then pursue the things that make for peace and build up the community.
> Romans 14:19

Taking their cue from the Vatican II *Declaration on Christian Education*, many documents describe a Catholic school as a 'faith community'.

A later document published by the Congregation for Catholic Education points out that here 'community' is a theological rather than a sociological one (though the latter dimension is presented as being very important).

We recognise that our faith community is in the process of formation.

Sometimes, the shortcomings we see around us may make us very sceptical about whether we will ever find faith *or* community.

Given the diversity of people's life stories, there are bound to be disagreements and crises. While a school is established to spread the faith and to foster efforts to live it, people come to these tasks with different backgrounds and preparedness.

The school is a way station for a pilgrim people. We should not be surprised or discouraged if it is not yet an exemplary community.

We acknowledge the faith and goodwill around us, hoping that all members of the school community, each according to their capacity, may pursue peace and the building of community.

Faith

> 'Paris is worth a Mass.'
> Henry IV of France (1553-1610)

In the sixteenth century, France was torn by religious wars. Henry, a claimant to the French throne, had been raised a Protestant but in 1593 converted to Catholicism because it was unthinkable that a Protestant could be king of France. He is said to have made the above comment to a friend, meaning that it was worth becoming a Catholic if that was the price that had to be paid to gain the throne.

Down through the ages, people have been martyred because of their devotion to the Mass. Less spectacularly, even today, many people go to Mass daily.

In his 1965 encyclical, *Mysterium Fidei*, Paul VI reminded us that 'the Eucharist is a very great mystery – in fact, properly speaking, in the words of the Sacred Liturgy, the mystery of Faith'. He went on to recall the description of the Mass by Leo XIII: 'It contains all supernatural realities in a remarkable richness and variety of miracles'.

Very properly, then, after the Consecration by proclaiming 'The Mystery of Faith', our Celebrant focuses our attention on the sublime reality that is being enacted.

We and our students could well adopt the plea to Our Lord: 'Lord, that I may see'.

Faith

> *Oasis*, n. an area in a desert made fertile by a source of water.

The Sahara desert is somewhat larger than Australia in area. Beneath the sand is a very large catchment of fresh water, which comes to the surface in places. Those who live in such localities dig wells and plant trees to protect the water from sand storms.

There are ninety oases in the Sahara, varying in size from townships to small encampments. They were, and are, important stopping points for travellers looking for fresh supplies and rest.

In our journey through life, the sacraments may be considered as oases, through which we gain strength and a sense of direction.

In our everyday life, and that of our students, the most common sacraments are Holy Communion and Reconciliation. In reality, many students' First Reconciliation is their last: priests may not be readily available or students do not see any point in the sacrament.

As they get older, they may receive the sacrament of Holy Orders or Matrimony. At times, circumstances may call for the Anointing of the Sick.

We know that sacraments are sources of the graces particularly suited to people's circumstances.

We strive to strengthen our faith in the sacraments and encourage our students to believe in them and frequent them.

Faith

> The confessional should not be a torture chamber.
> Pope Francis.

The confessional was indeed a torture chamber for Rudolph Miller in F. Scott Fitzgerald's short story, 'Absolution'. It was part of a draft of *The Great Gatsby* (1925), but discarded and published as a short story in 1924.

Rudolph's father, an inflexible and insensitive man, insists that Rudolph should go to Confession. The confessor is Father Schwartz, a man on the verge of a mental and emotional collapse.

Through nervousness, the eleven-year-old Rudolph tells a lie in Confession. He believes he has thus made a 'bad confession'. In this state, he is taken to Mass by his father and feels coerced into to receiving Holy Communion. He believes that he is now guilty of a sacrilege. Again off to Confession, he finds that Father Schwartz closes the grille before he can explain himself. Another 'bad confession!'

Rudolph now resolves, not that he will sin no more but that he will never again put 'abstraction before the necessities of his ease and comfort'.

Some people recount experiences like Rudolph's; others find Confession liberating and a source of peace.

For a variety of reasons, as one priest put it, there in not a 'flood of penitents' approaching the sacrament of Reconciliation these days. Chances are that the majority of those that do go are adults - gray haired perhaps.

As we rekindle our faith in this sacrament, we certainly need to help our students to develop a deeper understanding of the sacrament of Reconciliation as a source of forgiveness, grace and peace.

Faith

> At least let me meet my heavenly Lord in a better posture than in my bed.
>
> Charles II (1630-1685)

In accordance with the law, when Charles II assumed the British throne in 1660, he did so as a Protestant.

On his deathbed, he desired to become a Catholic. He was received into the Church by a Benedictine, Father John Huddleston, When the time came for the king to receive Holy Communion, he tried to get out of bed to show due reverence, only to be restrained by Huddleston, who reminded him that God reads the heart.

We encourage our students to approach the distribution of Holy Communion with reverence, and, having received Communion, to greet Our Lord in the words of St Richard of Chichester as Friend and Brother and to speak to him accordingly.

Faith

> [Jesus] then asked the father: 'How long is it since he had this affliction?' 'Ever since he was a child', he answered; 'and many a time the spirit threw him into the fire or into water to kill him. Oh, if you can do anything, take our trouble to heart and help us'. Jesus said to him: 'As to that "if you can do anything", one who believes can do everything'. The child's father at once cried out: 'I do believe! Help me if I do not!'
>
> Mark 9:21-25

Nothing is so heart-wrenching as the life-threatening illness of our children. In desperation, we feel prepared to try anything that will help them. We sense that in fact it was desperation – something of 'What have I got anything to lose?' – that led the boy's father to seek help from Jesus' disciples, and even from Jesus himself when he came upon the scene.

The father did his best to rise to the challenge Jesus offered: 'I do believe! Help me if I do not!'

As we face up to our own struggles, we may well find it helpful to repeat the prayer: 'I do believe! Help me if I do not!'

Faith

> Thereupon the disciples came up to Jesus and asked him privately: 'Why were we unable to drive him [a demon] out?' 'Because of your little faith', he replied; 'I tell you positively, if you have faith as small as a mustard seed, you may say to this hill, "Move away from here to there", and it will move away. Nothing will be impossible to you. As to this particular kind [of demon] it cannot be driven out except by prayer and fasting'.
>
> Matthew 17:19-21

How embarrassing for the apostles: despite all their efforts, they could not cast out the demon, and, by the time Jesus came along, the crowd of spectators was becoming restless.

At times, we have to deal with difficult students. Following Jesus' example, these are to be given special attention.

The apostles struggled in vain to deal with the tormented boy whom Jesus himself was then obliged to cure. When the apostles asked why, they were given the above reply.

There are few of us who have not felt defeated by some students.

It is to be noted that Jesus, while advocating prayer and fasting, also took decisive action.

We might pray for the insight to perceive and carry out the action that is needed to help troubled children.

Faith

> Now hearing the people talk about Jesus. she came along in the crowd behind and touched his garment. For she kept saying: 'If I but touch the hem of his garment I shall be well'. Instantly the source of her hemorrhage dried up and she felt the sensation of being permanently cured of her complaint... whereupon he said to her: 'Daughter, your faith has cured you. Go home and be at peace'.
>
> Mark 5:28-30, 34

How often Jesus told people that their faith had saved them.

He had the capacity to arouse the belief that God could, would, and wanted to intervene in a healing manner in a person's life.

Jesus had the ability not only to arouse this belief but also to help people to reach out in a way that was previously impossible for them. In this case, it was not so much to touch Jesus' clothes, as to openly acknowledge her condition in confidence that a cure was possible.

With the grace of God, teachers and schools can also arouse this kind of saving faith. Sometimes, the child makes the first faltering step on the road to healing – not always on the road to a cure. We can but act as agents.

It would be a wonderful farewell if a school could say to students 'Be of good heart, your faith has made you whole. Go in peace'.

Faith

If we've read *The Catcher in the Rye*, we will recall Holden Caulfield's hatred for what he called 'phonies'.

We know that children can spot a phony at a hundred paces: they can see whether teachers really believe what they are talking about.

Children pick up on the vague or unconvinced and unconvincing explanation and the implied or stated reservations.

We recall the words of the first epistle of St Peter that we will always have an answer ready for people who ask the reason for our faith.

Faith

> He then took hold of a little child, placed it in front of them, and folding it in his arms said to them: 'Whoever befriends one of these little children in my name, befriends me, and he who befriends me befriends not me but him whose ambassador I am'.
>
> Mark 9:37

The mother of a fifteen-year-old boy relates that one night she looked in on her sleeping son; he was so totally obnoxious she had to draw on all her reserves as a mother to say 'No matter what, I love you!'

How much harder it was for his teachers (who were not fortified by a mother's love) to deal with the boy! In all seriousness, some teachers wondered whether the boy was human. (Happily, the boy has grown into a successful and amiable man.)

On the other hand, some children we teach are very easy to love.

Hard or easy, faith sees all children in the way that Jesus expressed above. It is not just a striking comparison, but a reality.

We need faith to see Jesus in all the children we teach.

Faith

> O God save me; see how the waters close about me shoulder high! I am like one who sticks fast in deep mire, with no ground under his feet, one who has ventured out into mid-ocean to be drowned by the storm.
>
> Psalm 69:1-2

At times, it can feel like this! Our troubles seem to pile up.

We may be sick, or have family concerns, or difficulty in a relationship, or money troubles, or unhappiness at work ... or all of the above.

On top of our troubles, we have to keep going with our classes, without feeling enthusiasm or inclination.

Our faith teaches us that we will be given the strength to deal with our problems.

Sometimes, we may have our faith tested to the limit, like Peter the Great of Russia (1682-1721). As he lay dying, he suffered excruciating pain and his conscience was burdened with terrible crimes; despite all, he hung on with the prayer 'I believe and I hope'.

Faith

> But have courage, I have overcome the world.
>
> John 16:33

One of Frederick Faber's hymns contains the lines 'this rough-spoken world, where the banners of darkness are boldly unfurled'.

'Darkness' can denote forces of evil active in the world.

The novelist Joseph Conrad used the metaphor 'the heart of darkness' to describe people's capacity for evil.

More recently in popular culture, Darth Vader spoke of 'the power of the dark side'.

We know of the evils that fester in the dark web.

The theologian Donatien Mollat has explained the meaning of this dark 'world':

> ... a formidable power of negation and refusal, which exceeds human limits and plunges its roots into a dark centre of hatred and lies... [it] demonstrates at what depth salvation intervenes, what struggles it must face, what an abyss of pride and rebellion it must overcome.

When evils seem insurmountable, we need faith to believe that Jesus has really plumbed the abyss and overcome the powers of darkness.

Faith

> It is a far, far better thing that I do, than I have ever done; it is a far, far better rest that I go to than I have ever known.
> Sydney Carton, in *A Tale of Two Cities*.

We can probably remember reading this novel during our school days. We recall that Carton resembled Charles Darnay so closely that it was possible for him to take the latter's place at the guillotine.

It was a singular act of generosity.

Although he seasoned his comments with biblical quotations, Carton was far from being portrayed as a religious man, a man of faith.

This character is a reminder that religious people, people of faith, do not have a monopoly on selflessness, generosity and heroism.

We aspire to be people of faith, but we recognise the good accomplished by many people who disclaim any religious motivation.

We thank God for the many ways in which good is accomplished.

Faith

> I fear that Jesus will go by and that I will not recognise him, that the Lord will pass by my side in one of the little people in need and I will not realise it is Jesus.
>
> St Augustine

Some people assert that it is the 'deserving poor', the 'good kids', that we must help. Often, the deserving poor will express their gratitude and we may have the good fortune to see our work producing improvements. We thank God.

What of the 'undeserving poor'? – those who seem to take advantage of all the help they receive and yet seem to reject everything we stand for.

Such circumstances test our faith and our mettle.

Faith

> To listen, to reason, to propose.

In its 2019 document *Male and Female he created them: towards a path of dialogue on the question of gender theory in education*, The Congregation for Catholic Education suggests this strategy to underpin a Christian education, which, rooted in faith, will direct the mind to solutions that are truly human.

Gender theory, artificial intelligence… the world our students are going into: they need our help and example to develop a strong faith and a generous mind to engage in dialogue without surrendering principle.

Faith

> To know God and to understand his ways and to watch in his presence in all sanctity is the greatest end of life,
>
> Matt Talbot (1856-1925)

From the time he left school aged twelve until he was thirty, this Dublin man drank heavily. He became an alcoholic, spending his wages on alcohol, often selling possessions, stealing, borrowing, to support his habit.

One night, when he was broke, he stood outside a pub hoping to be invited in for a drink. When no one offered, he decided to give up drinking by taking a pledge not to drink. Later, he said that it is easier to raise someone from the dead than for an alcoholic to reform. Recovering alcoholics vouch for this statement.

Searching for a deeper understanding of his beliefs, he began to read extensively with the help of a spiritual guide. He went to Mass daily and spent much of his spare time in prayer.

He worked diligently as a labourer, lived frugally and was generous in sharing the little he had. He made sure to pay back the money he had borrowed and to compensate those whom he had robbed.

His was a lived faith.

Faith

> Blessed be the God and Father of our Lord Jesus Christ, the merciful father who is the source of unalloyed comfort, and continues to comfort us in every affliction, that we may in turn be enabled to comfort those who are in any kind of affliction...
>
> 2 Corinthians 1: 3-4

When we recite the Creed, the first article is belief in God the Father Almighty. As St Paul points out, God is a merciful (some translations say 'tender') Father.

Too often, perhaps stoical observance of commandments can blind us to the truth that God is a loving father and that keeping commandments is a loving response. Moreover, we move beyond ourself to care for others who are also God's children.

We try to nurture in our students a faith that draws its strength from love and responding to love. As St John reminds us: we love God because he has loved us first.

3

On being called: the place where we belong

> He established some as apostles, and some as inspired prophets, others again as evangelists, and others as pastors and teachers, thus organising the saints for the work of the ministry, which consists in building up the body of Christ, until we all attain to unity in faith and deep knowledge of the Son of God.
> Ephesians 4:11-13.

Faith tells us that Providence assigns to each person a role that they are free to accept or reject. That is: each person is called to make a specific contribution, sometimes small, sometimes large, to human history.

We are called to make our contribution as teachers.

Called

> 'You talkin' to me?'
> Travis Bickle in Martin Scorsese's *Taxi Driver* (1976)

Robert De Nero, acting as the disturbed Travis Bickle, is looking at himself in a mirror. No one is talking to him and no one is calling him.

A priest. who by his own admission was something of an introvert and a man of modest talents, had been assured before he went to the seminary that there were people who would one day talk to him, depending on his ministry. He doubted whether anyone would talk to him or call him. He struggled with his studies but kept going, clinging to assurances.

Not long after his ordination, he was travelling on a tram which had been stopped because of an accident. A crowd had gathered around a badly-injured man; he may have been dying The young priest got off the tram and made his way over to the crowd, who parted to let him through. He knelt and gave the man conditional absolution. At that moment, he believed that Someone had been talking to him and had really called him.

He remained introverted and a man of modest talents, but ever available to those who asked for his help.

Called

> God has created me to do him some definite service; He has committed some work to me which he has not committed to another. I have my mission: I may never know it in this life, but I shall be told it in the next. I have a part in a great work; I am a link in a chain, a bond of connection between persons. He has not created me for naught. I shall do good, I shall do his work: I shall be an angel of peace, a preacher of truth in my own place, while not intending it, if I do but keep his commandments and serve him in my calling.
>
> John Henry Newman (1801-1890)

Most people would probably agree that John Henry Newman was called to make a large contribution to human history, as a scholar, controversialist, preacher and religious leader; and now as a saint.

An original thinker, he had the gift of expressing truths simply and memorably.

His works have been very influential, enlightening and affecting many people,

We seek an ever-deeper conviction of God's loving plan for us, and its connection with his loving plan for others.

Called

> And now the Lord said to Moses, Here is the name of the man that I have singled out to help you, Bezalel,. I have filled him with my divine spirit, making him wise, adroit and skilful in every kind of craftsmanship, so that he can design whatever is to be designed in gold, silver, and bronze, and carve both stone and jewel and wood of all sorts.
>
> Exodus 31:1-6.

About a year after the Israelites left Egypt, Moses gave instructions for the making of the Ark of the Covenant, and the Tent which was to house it. The Ark was an acacia wood chest 1.3 metres long, .8 of a metre wide and .8 of a metre high. It was plated with gold inside and out and its ornate lid held representations of angels. The Ark contained the tablets of the Law, the rod of Aaron and a jar of manna. The lid was called the Mercy Seat, the site of *kabod*, the power and presence of YHWH.

The task of fashioning the Ark fell to Bezalel, who had been endowed with appropriate gifts.

We will be aware of many of our gifts, though there are most certainly others of which we are unaware. Sometimes, they are discovered by accident or through the need to respond to unexpected demands.

Our gifts determine the type of service we can render and they impress our individuality on our teaching.

We might reflect on our gifts, thanking God for them and asking for the grace to use them in the way he wishes.

Called

> ... the spirit yields a harvest of love, joy, peace, patience, kindness, generosity, forbearance, gentleness, faith, courtesy, temperateness, purity.
>
> Galatians 5:22

These qualities are traditionally called the Fruits of the Holy Spirit. We are possibly more familiar with the Seven Gifts of the Holy Spirit: wisdom, understanding, counsel, fortitude, knowledge, piety and the fear of the Lord – whether by these or other names.

We know that in Baptism and in Confirmation, we receive a share of these Gifts.

Just as we have an individual range of talents, so too the Spirit endows us with a specific spiritual profile to support us in the role that Providence has assigned us. Spiritual gifts find expression in human interaction, as Abbot Marmion reminds us: God formed within our Lady a mother's heart fit to raise her Son.

We thank the Holy Spirit for the gifts we have received, and ask for a greater awareness of them.

Called

> Gladly, therefore, will I boast of my infirmities, that the power of Christ may spread a sheltering cover over me... for when I am weak then I am strong.
> 2 Corinthians 12:9-10

Our gifts and strengths are defining influences in our lives; so are our limitations.

No matter how hard we try, we may never run a four-minute mile, compose a symphony to equal one by Mozart, or be declared teacher of the year.

Some of our colleagues may appear so versatile, or are so outstanding in some aspect of our profession that we may feel demoralised.

It would appear that there is great wisdom in accepting our limitations, and, having done our best to deal with them, to be at peace.

We can be certain that, if we do our best, Providence will arrange things so that through the combination of our strengths and weaknesses, there will be one or more students whose hearts only we can touch. All teachers have their own little flock.

We accept others' giftedness graciously and accept our limitations gracefully so that the power of Christ may spread a sheltering cover over us.

Called

> Part of education is to teach children how to play because you learn how to be social through games and you learn the joy of life.
>
> Pope Francis

These words are part of the short speech the Pope made when he announced the winner of the 2016 Global Teacher Prize, which is sponsored by the Varkey Foundation, founded by the educational entrepreneur Sonny Varkey in 2010.

The prize of $1,000,000 attracts entrants from all over the world. In 2016, it was won by Hanan Al Hroubi, a teacher in a town near Ramallah, capital of the Palestinian State.

She had planned to train as an interpreter, but when her studies were interrupted by civil unrest, she found herself in the classroom where the violence children saw outside the school influenced their behaviour inside it.

She devised a highly-successful strategy based on play to counteract the violence that children witnessed.

Her calling, unimagined in her teens, was made known to her by the circumstances in which she found herself.

Perhaps some our students may need help in discerning the calling that may lie hidden in their circumstances.

Called

> Blessed be the God and Father of our Lord Jesus Christ, who in Christ has blessed us with every manner of spiritual blessing in the heavenly realm. These blessings correspond to his choice of us in Christ before the foundation of the world, that we should be holy and without blemish in his sight. Out of love, he predestined us for himself to become through Jesus Christ his adopted children...
>
> Ephesians 1:3-5

Over and above our call to *do* we have a call to *be* and to be *transformed*.

As St Paul reminds us, before the world began, from eternity, we have been in God's mind, and chosen not merely to live a human life but to share his life as his children.

When we think about this call, we may feel a sense of wonder, almost of disbelief, before so great a mystery. We reflect that God has things to say to us that he will not say to any other person, because, although we share this destiny with others, we are unique and uniquely loved. In fact, as *Revelations* implies (2:17), God has a personal name for each of us, known to himself, and eventually, to be shared only with us.

Called

> I shall pass this way but once, any good, therefore, that I can do or any kindness that I can show to any human being, let me do it now. Let me not defer or neglect it, for I shall not pass this way again.
>
> Dale Carnegie

Dale Carnegie (1888-1955) was a pioneer in delivering courses that help people to make the most of their potential. His book *How to Make Friends and Influence People* was an instant best seller when published in the 1930s and the book and his courses remain popular.

This quotation is obviously directed not at maximising our potential but at helping our neighbour. It is a useful reminder. It is a supplement to the old saying: 'Whoever who gives quickly gives twice'.

St Mary MacKillop recommended that we never leave a good deed undone.

Called

On a battlefield during World War II, an Anglican priest approached a Catholic priest saying that he wanted to become a Catholic.

The Catholic priest remonstrated: 'This is not the time to make such a decision. So many people depend on you. You have the duty to stay and look after them. If we both survive, come and see me after the war and we'll take things from there'.

They both survived and the two men met. The Catholic priest advised the Anglican to make a retreat. 'Where?' 'Look up the phone book.' The Anglican did so: he picked a monastery (seemingly) at random, went there, became a Catholic and afterwards a Catholic priest.

Some people have never wanted to be anything but a teacher. Others have found their way into teaching because nothing else seemed to be available. No doubt, there are others who have taken up teaching after a number of other jobs.

Whatever our personal story, here and now we have a class that we have to do our best to teach,

We are grateful for the action of Providence in our lives, trusting for the strength to fulfil our obligations

Called

> As he re-entered the boat, the man previously possessed asked leave to stay with him, but instead of permitting him, Jesus said to him: 'Go home to your people and relate to them all the Lord has done out of sheer pity for you'.
>
> Mark 5:18-19

The Gospels paint a terrifying picture of this man who roamed naked among the tombs, howling, cutting himself with stones, and breaking the manacles that were put on him.

When Jesus had cured him, he was seen clothed and sitting, talking to Jesus.

The cured demoniac felt called to accompany Jesus, but such was not his vocation.

Jesus arranged the man's call to suit his circumstances and those of his people. Moreover, this was a cure effected without a stirring up of the victim's faith – his condition prevented it. The man's mission was to announce what had been done, not in response to faith, but out of sheer pity. Evidently, Jesus believed that this was the message the man's people required.

Vocation has a personal and social dimension.

We might consider the personal qualities of our own calling, and thanking God for them, consider how we can put then at the disposal of other people.

Called

> Do not flatter yourself that a royal court will shelter you in the general massacre of your countrymen. Keep silence, and the Jews will find some other means of deliverance; on you and yours destruction will fall. Who knows but you have reached the throne only to be ready for such an opportunity as this?
>
> Esther 4:14-15

Most probably, the writer of *Esther* set it in the time of the Persian king Xerxes, around 470 BC. In this book, where Xerxes is called Ahasuerus, intrigues at his court had stirred up a persecution of the Jews.

Esther was the niece and adopted daughter of a Jew called Mordecai. We are told 'Beauty was hers of form and face'. She was a member of a group of girls selected to be groomed in the royal court, with the possibility that one of them might be chosen as a successor to a banished queen. The choice eventually fell on Esther, who managed to remain faithful to her religion and also to plead with the king for her people.

Mordecai was able to point out that her gifts and position were likely to impose a special calling on her.

It is one of the privileges of teachers to help students to perceive their gifts; if the occasion presents itself we might also suggest a calling to which they appear to be fitted.

Called

> ... we must remember that teachers and educators fulfil a specific Christian vocation and share an equally specific participation in the mission of the Church, to the extent that 'it depends chiefly on them whether the Catholic school achieves its purpose'.
> Congregation for Catholic Education, *The Catholic School on the Threshold of the Third Millennium*, 1997, para.19.

As the quotation asserts, teachers in Catholic schools have a vocation that involves them in the mission of the Church. The extract includes a quotation of an earlier publication, *The Catholic School*, (1977). It reminds us that the school cannot achieve its purpose without us.

In this context, we might recall that the Bishop of the diocese is therein the chief teacher of the faith; our authority to teach Religion is delegated by him.

We may feel unworthy of the calling, but we are where God has called us to be.

We might thank God for the privilege he has given us; we might also pray for our Bishop and we might ask for the grace to be true to our calling.

Called

> No man is an island entire of itself, every man is a piece of the continent...
> John Donne, *Meditation XVII*

John Donne, Anglican priest and poet, memorably expressed people's connection, one with another.

This connection is demonstrated in the lives of three people: Catherine de Hueck Doherty, Eddie Doherty and Joseph Raya.

Catherine de Hueck (1896-1985), born into Russian minor nobility, was forced to flee during the revolution, served as a nurse during World War I, and entered Canada as a refugee. She became a sought-after and affluent lecturer. Seeking more in life, she began to work among the marginalised, first in Harlem and later in Ontario, where she established Madonna House.

Eddie Doherty (1890-1975) was a successful journalist and scriptwriter. He experienced sorrow in that his first wife died in an epidemic and his second in an accident. He went to interview Catherine. He became impressed with her and her work and she became the third Mrs Doherty. Late in his life, he was ordained priest in the Melkite Rite, where priests are allowed to marry.

He was ordained by Joseph Raya (1916-2005), a Lebanese Melkite Bishop. After ordination as a priest, he was sent to Cairo; there his outspoken defence of women led to his expulsion. He was then sent to Birmingham, Alabama, where he became friends with Martin Luther King, and was beaten up by the Klan. He opened the first Melkite church for African Americans. He was then appointed to Israel, befriending Moslems, Christians and Jews with the same embrace. He once declared to the Knesset that the Israelis were treating the Palestinians in the way the Nazis had treated them. He retired to Canada, where he was very impressed by the Dohertys' work and the spirituality developed at Madonna House. He was also friends with the scripture scholar, Father Francis Martin, adviser to Cardinal Suenens at Vatican II.

Perhaps our network is not so notable, but we are involved in a mesh of relationships – with our families, friends, colleagues and students – which influences us, and which we influence in return.

Called

> As Jesus went on from there, he noticed a man at a counter in the tax gatherer's office – Matthew was his name – and said to him: 'Follow me'. At that, the man quit his business and became one of his followers.
>
> Matthew 9:9

Michelangelo da Caravaggio (1571-1610), usually known as Caravaggio, painted this scene in 1600. It can be viewed on Google and repays close attention.

Matthew and others are counting money when Jesus appears and points to him. Matthew still has one hand on the money and points to himself, as if he cannot believe that he is the one being called. Other characters remain engrossed in counting while other spectators wonder what is going on.

We may find it hard to believe that we are called like Matthew to be associated with Jesus in spreading the good news.

Perhaps we were employed as a science teacher and asked to take an RE class, as task for which we feel ourselves unsuited. Or maybe we have been asked to accompany students on a retreat, when such an experience is foreign to us. Or as an art teacher we are asked to supervise children in painting a religious mural based on religious theme which we do not understand. Or we find ourselves taking a small group to Reconciliation, a sacrament we have not received for a very long time.

Or maybe we have always felt we were called to teach in a Catholic school.

Or we may consider Walter J Ciszek (1904-1984) a Jesuit priest who was working in Russia when, on a trumped-up charge, he was convicted of spying. He was sentenced to 20 years' imprisonment: 5 in the Lubyanka and then 15 years in gulags, some in the Arctic circle. He worked in mines, factories and other unexpected places. He concluded that God's 'will for us was in the 24 hours of each day: the people, the places, the circumstances he sets before us in that time'.

Regardless of our background, for us – in Ciszek's terms – our setting today is the classroom, with the young people, colleagues and parents that we are called to interact with.

4

On dedication: being there for the long haul

> ... it seemed that the bush was alight, yet did not burn. Here is a great sight, said Moses, I must go up and see more of it, a bush that does not waste by burning.
>
> Exodus 2:2-3

The fire described in Exodus was robust and enduring: qualities that are applicable to the exercise of 'dedication' or of similar terms like enthusiasm, zeal, commitment, keenness or perseverance.

'Dedication' leads teachers to be there for the long haul, to be genuinely interested in their work and to stimulate their students.

While there are a fortunate few who are constantly buoyed up by excitement, many, if not most, of us find that our enthusiasm is at times put to the test. It is then that faith and a sense of vocation help us to continue as dedicated professionals.

Albert Schweitzer wisely observed that there is a need for a sober enthusiasm rather than a passing emotional engagement.

Dedication

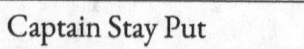
Captain Stay Put

This was the title the public conferred on Captain Kurt Carlsen (1914-1989).

He was master of the Swedish-American cargo ship SS *Flying Enterprise*, which left Hamburg for New York in December 1951.

The vessel was caught in a gale and tossed by fifty-foot waves which caused the ship to list to such an extent that Carlsen ordered the crew and passengers to abandon ship. This was a hazardous maneuver in which one person was killed. Carlsen, believing that his ship could be saved, stayed aboard. A tugboat dispatched from Falmouth eventually was able to secure a towline and began to tow the Flying Enterprise. Pictures of Carlsen on the craft and ultimately on the upturned hull were flashed around the world. The drama went on for thirteen days until a monster wave caused the ship to sink – about 60 kilometres from shore and safety. Carlsen had to jump into the winter sea; he was rescued by the tugboat.

When he arrived in New York, he was given a ticker tape parade: his courage was recognised there and through messages received from all around the world.

A hero, no doubt. We know of many others less celebrated, who day after day, week after week, look after the chronically ill, or support the reclusive and the aged or bear patiently with their children who seem to go out of their way to hurt them, or teachers who just get on with it...

Dedication

> Go and heal the sick...
> Matthew 10:8

Three Australian doctors have answered this call admirably.

Catherine and Richard Hamlin, gynecologists and devout Anglicans, went from Sydney to Ethiopia in 1959 to help women who had been injured in childbirth. They set up clinics and remained working there for the remainder of their professional life – Catherine lived to be 93.

Mary Glowrey, highly qualified with a successful gynecological practice in Melbourne, felt called to work as a medical missionary in India. In 1920, she sailed for India and joined the Sisters of Jesus, Mary and Joseph. As Sister Mary of the Sacred Heart, she worked as a gynecologist, helping Indian women and training midwives and nurses for the next thirty-seven years without returning to Australia.

Their dedication was robust and enduring.

Dedication

When Ruth retired after forty years in the classroom, it could then justly be said of her that she was as enthusiastic about her teaching as she had been when she first stepped into class.

Her enthusiasm was obvious in her geniality to parents and colleagues, her genuine love for her students, her thorough lesson preparation, her helpful review of students' responses and the genuine excitement she aroused in her students.

There must have been days when she was sick, troubled and worn out, yet she had evidently resolved to leave these circumstances at the classroom door.

We might think about the level of our enthusiasm and pray that the Lord who said that he had come to cast fire on the earth will help us to rekindle and maintain our keenness.

Dedication

Some of us are born extroverts who enjoy the dramatic. Others of us are introverts, who prefer the low-key approach. Some of us are gregarious; others of us are reserved.

It would obviously be quite foolish to try to make ourselves into something that we cannot feel comfortable with or sustain.

Our commitment will go hand in hand with our personal style, which we will continue throughout our professional life to develop and improve.

It has long been accepted as a sound proposition that grace builds on nature. The disposition that we have inherited and grown into is a point where God will meet us, work with us and cherish us.

We strive to know ourselves, accept ourselves, and develop the positive qualities that we can practise with integrity.

Dedication

> ... there is an evil bitter zeal that cuts us off from God.
>
> St Benedict

There is no shortage of examples of misdirected religious enthusiasm. For instance, it is recorded that, in the early days of monasticism, monks used to burst forth from a certain monastery armed with clubs they called 'Israels': their purpose was to use the clubs to thrash anyone whose fervour they found deficient.

We can also cite the jurist who believed that the fires under heretics should be kept low so that they had a half-hour's practice for the fires of hell.

Violence – physical or emotional – can never be justified as a means of glorifying God.

A former student – and a former Catholic – recalls the day when his teacher slammed his face into the blackboard. Unfortunately for the teacher, she had forgotten that the board was mounted on horizontal swivels so that the force applied to the bottom sent the top of the board crashing down on her head. She was felled, to the cheers of her pupils.

Similarly, officious promotion of religion and unjustified or unwholesome prying into children's backgrounds cannot be countenanced; invariably, these strategies will be counterproductive.

Perhaps, we have sometimes allowed a faulty enthusiasm to carry us away.

We can reflect on James' and John's suggestion that they call down fire from heaven on unbelieving towns and recall the way Jesus dampened down their misplaced enthusiasm and indignation.

We seek the wisdom to direct our energies constructively.

Dedication

> Beloved, believe not every spirit, but try the spirits whether they be of God.
>
> 1 John 4:1

Lord Longford, who died in 2001 aged 95, spent a lifetime fighting for those he considered victims of oppression.

A convert to Catholicism, he took seriously the Church's social justice teachings. Among his other activities, he frequently visited those in prison, including Myra Hindley, who was involved in the Yorkshire Moor murders of little children. His campaign for her parole embroiled him in controversy.

This quest, and others he undertook, led some people to believe he was naïve or misguided.

Few denied his faith, sincerity and commitment.

His career serves as a reminder that none of us is infallible, and even our most zealous activities need to be embarked on only after prayer and careful reflection.

We reflect on the source of our enthusiasm for good causes seeking whether it is inspired by God and not by whims, delusions or obsessions.

Dedication

People in caring professions like teaching are prone to burnout.

This condition can affect totally-committed people who consistently give their all and particularly if they are dealing with difficult cases.

People who feel they are suffering from burnout will be well be advised to speak to a person of sound judgment who has the genuine capacity to help. If people are not qualified to help, then the sufferer will be like the Ancient Mariner, forced to repeat the story over and over again, only to find that therein there is no relief.

Women and men suffering from burnout may feel that they are wrong to take a break; they may feel that they are deserting their post. Calmer thinking will help them to see that their work is not meant to destroy them.

We may be in a position to help a colleague who is sinking; perhaps we can shoulder some of his or her load, or put in a good word for them.

We pray for colleagues who are at the end of their tether.

Dedication

> Cared for in life and death

Dorothy Day (1897-1980) was an American laywoman who lived a life of intense commitment to the Gospel through the press, activism and practical service to the poor.

Speaking of the down and out men who sought shelter and lived in her Houses of Hospitality, she explained that the men were also given a burial and remembered in prayer.

She is an excellent exemplar of sustained zealous service.

We thank God for people like Dorothy Day, and ask for the grace to remain committed to the service to which he has called us.

Dedication

> For myself, I would have the whole people prophesy, with the spirit of the Lord resting on them too.
> Numbers 11:29

Moses had gathered seventy elders in a half circle at the tabernacle door. God shared with each of them some of the spirit which rested on Moses. Immediately, the elders began to prophesy. Two of the elders selected had not gone to the tabernacle but they too began to prophesy. Joshua, Moses' favourite servant, wanted to stop them, but, in the words recorded above, Moses was happy to let them continue.

It is to be hoped that the enthusiasm we bring to our work will be catching, and that our students develop an enthusiasm for learning and for working for the good of the community.

Dedication

> If we were transported with zeal, it was for God...
> Love for Christ impels us.
>
> 2 Corinthians 5:14

Zeal and innovation have been hallmarks of Catholic teachers since the first popular school was established in 1599. It was daring to take urchins, put them in a classroom and teach them. Only zealous persons could have done it.

Marguerite Bourgeoys (1620-1700) exemplified the zeal that has inspired generations of teachers to respond intuitively to local conditions. As a young woman, she saw girls being taught by the Nuns founded by Alix Leclerq in France in 1597. Because of Church practices at the time, the Nuns were unable to leave the cloister and lay people like Marguerite banded together to teach children unable to attend the school.

An official from the new colony in Canada visited France and invited Marguerite to teach children in Canada. She agreed and settled in Ville-Marie (which eventually became Montreal). She worked among the poor until someone gave her a stable to use as a school.

She was joined by other women and together they became the nucleus of a Religious congregation. Determined that the Sisters would not be confined to the cloister, she travelled to France to plead her case with Louis XIV. He agreed and expressed his admiration for her.

Using this flexibility, she established a boarding school, a vocational school and made attempts to provide schooling for First Nations people.

We witness many of our colleagues who are enthusiastic and inventive like Marguerite Bourgeoys.

Dedication

> We hope to be found occupied in the tasks God has given us.

The writer and academic C. S. Lewis (1898-1963) endorsed this approach to life.

When we were younger, many of us would have read his *The Lion the Witch and the Wardrobe*.

He was raised an Anglican, abandoned belief for a while but then regained it with such conviction that he wrote a number of popular religious books,

We all hope to share Lewis' understanding that one's gifts point the way to work effectively with sustained commitment.

Dedication

> 'A Kemble drink'

This saying, the equivalent of 'one for the road,' owes its origin to St John Kemble (1599-1679).

In his time, and for more than a hundred years, being a Catholic priest had been a capital offence in England. Some priests who returned there secretly were captured on arrival; others were arrested after a short time. Kemble managed to minister as a priest for fifty-four years, winning the esteem of Protestants and Catholics. He was falsely implicated in a bogus plot, and although exonerated, he was condemned as a Catholic priest.

Those who came to lead him to execution were depressed by their task. He asked for time to pray and then, to cheer them he invited them to join him in a last pipe and a glass of wine: the Kemble drink.

Revered by all as 'a great gentleman', he was found at his post, brave and dedicated to the last.

Dedication

> Unto death

Leonard Cheshire VC, OM (1917-1992) and Sue Ryder CMG, OBE (1924-2000) were celebrated for their achievements during World War II as well as for their work in peacetime.

Before their wedding in 1959, they pledged themselves to find God in the sick, the unwanted and the dying. They undertook to follow this calling 'unto death'.

Their work continues in the Foundations and Homes they established.

The many honours they received did not distract them from the work to which they had dedicated their lives.

5

On co-operation: working in association with our colleagues

> Two things must never leave you: kindness and loyalty; let these be seals that hang about your neck, so to both God and people you will be friend and confidant.
>
> Proverbs 3:3-4

Inspired by faith, called to teach and dedicated to the work within their classrooms and other learning areas, teachers do not operate alone: unless they are stationed in a one-teacher school, teachers work in association with colleagues – collegiality is a hallmark. of our profession.

While it is true that some teachers like to work in isolation, schools cannot survive if such behaviour is the norm. For their personal and professional well-being, and for the good of the school, teachers need to work in association with each other with kindness and loyalty: in the words of Proverbs, to be friends and confidants.

Co-operation

> But those behind cried 'Forward'
> And those before cried 'Back'
> And backward now and forward
> Wavered the deep array...
> Lord Macaulay, *Lays of Ancient Rome* (1842)

Macaulay is relating the heroic stand of the legendary Roman, Horatio.

Around 509 BC, the Romans expelled their king and the Republic was born. According to one legend, an ally of the deposed king attacked Rome, catching the militia unaware. Horatio and two comrades stood fast at a bridge until the troops were able to re-enter the city.

The bravery of Horatio and his comrades completely unnerved the attacking column, so that contradictory commands were given and the column wavered.

Perhaps, we may have been fortunate enough to witness a modern-day Horatio making a principled stand.

It is also likely that we have come across organisations – schools included – where the main thrust is lost because of internal bickering.

Co-operation

> Come and take your full share in the meetings and in deliberating for the common good.
> From a letter attributed to St Barnabas (a companion of the Apostles).

'There is a Staff meeting today.' Few words are more likely to disturb the peace of staff members.

Those who address meetings often feel that they are speaking to the statues on Easter Island, while those who sit and listen may feel that they are suffering the death of a thousand cuts.

There may be one or two people who dominate procedures, those who have their all-too-familiar hobbyhorses, those who cannot contain themselves once they have the floor, or power brokers who, while not speaking, determine what is to be done, who is to be supported and who is to be left out to dry.

There may be an elephant in the room that no one wants to talk about.

Nevertheless, there are tasks which need to be explained and explored, initiatives that need to be assessed, colleagues who need to be affirmed.

It is obvious that any organisation will be more effective if its members are like minded.

We might consider our contributions to staff meetings and pray for the grace to deliberate for the common good.

Co-operation

> Let no-one despise your youth.
>
> I Timothy 4:12
>
> Be not harsh in rebuking an elderly man, but exhort him as you would a father. Treat young men as brothers, elderly women as mothers, younger women as sisters, with perfect charity.
>
> I Timothy 5:1-2

The staff of a school can be as diverse as the community at Ephesus over which Timothy presided.

There may be those starting out who are struggling to establish themselves.

Others, who are established and teach with ease, may well be asking themselves, 'Is this all there is?' They may be considering another career.

Some may have become jaded, looking upon everything with a jaundiced eye.

Without doubt, there will be dreadnoughts, who are neither swamped nor deflected from their course.

There may be teachers who feel defeated, but compelled, for financial reasons, to struggle on until retirement.

As co-workers, we owe our colleagues generous support, patience and understanding.

We are mindful of members of our staff, be they teachers or those who perform other, but no less important, tasks.

Co-operation

> As an obedient man I protest.
> Robert Grosseteste (1168-1253)

Grosseteste, Bishop of Lincoln, was a scholar, reformer and scientist. He died with a reputation for holiness, though he was never canonised.

Although he was loyal to the papacy, he voiced a disagreement about procedures face-to-face with the Pope. He understood that sometimes loyalty demands respectful dissent.

Sometimes, we need to help a colleague with advice. It may happen that we need to suggest to administrators a needed improvement.

These actions are not easy to do. They require courage and tact.

Co-operation

> There is a special providence in the fall of a sparrow.
> *Hamlet.*

Poor Hamlet! 'Punish'd' as he was 'with a sore distraction', he yet understood the scriptural notion that Providence is active in our lives.

And it is a benign Providence: a person is worth more than a flock of sparrows, and even the hairs of our head are numbered.

This concept is comforting for us, but it is also a reminder that Providence is equally, lovingly, involved in the life of our colleagues, those who are our friends, and those who are not close to us.

Co-operation

> ... in love serve one another. Why, the whole law is fulfilled by the observance of one precept. 'You shall love your neighbour as yourself'.
> Galatians 5:13-14

How easy to say, how hard to put into practice.

We readily enough rise to the occasion when our colleagues suffer a bereavement, or when there is occasion for celebrating a birth, engagement or marriage.

It is harder day-after-day to share our resources and expertise, to keep common facilities tidy, not to hog scarce resources, to turn up on time to relieve someone on yard duty, to meet deadlines so that others can complete common tasks, to be courteous to those to whom we are not close...

We are grateful for the consideration that others show to us, and try to be consistently alert to others' needs.

Co-operation

> But if you bite and devour one another, take heed, or you will be consumed by one another.
>
> Galatians 5:15

One of the French philosophers considered that 'hell is other people'.

This is an extreme statement of the obvious fact that it is not easy living in close contact with others.

In some staffrooms, criticism is as common as coffee, and life can indeed be something of a hell.

We might pray for the strength to bite our tongues when tempted to criticise others, and not to be part of a culture that nourishes dissension.

Co-operation

> And next, he [Judas Maccabe] must concern himself with the altar of burnt sacrifice that was now all defiled. And it was good counsel they took, the altar must be destroyed... So destroy it they did, and laid up the stones in a place apt for the purpose, there on the temple hill. Here they must remain until the coming of a prophet that should give sentence, what was to be done with them.
>
> 1 Maccabees 4:44-46

When Alexander the Great died, his kingdom was divided into several sections. One part, known as the Seleucid Empire, included Judea. Around 170 BC, the king ordered the Jews to worship his gods and he despoiled the Temple.

The brothers Maccabee led a revolt and reclaimed the Temple.

Judas, one of the brothers, was neither priest nor prophet, but it was his duty to lead his people in unprecedented circumstances. The Temple had been defiled and was to be restored; the altar previously consecrated with great solemnity presented a problem: what should they do in the absence of a direct message from God?

Judas and his followers deliberated and came up with the solution described above. They did what they thought was best, but had the humility to recognise their limitations.

The situations in which schools find themselves are always evolving, particularly in times of rapid social change.

Honest deliberations, where people contribute their insights to the best of their ability, will help a staff to devise strategies to suit local circumstances. At the same time, people will acknowledge that, while their solution is not perfect, it is the best they can do.

Co-operation

Apparently, in her early days in the convent, St Teresa of Avila was not always an exemplary Nun.

However, it is said that when people saw her in a group, they could rest assured that their reputation was safe: she would not tolerate unkind comments about others.

Teachers constantly find themselves in contact with others: colleagues, parents, students. It is inevitable that friction will sometimes arise. As human beings, we may imagine that our difficulties with others will be solved if we criticise them. Experience teaches us that criticism, far from solving a problem, can make it worse.

St James reflected that 'Human ingenuity is able to tame and has tamed every kind of beast and bird, reptile and sea animal, but no-one can tame the tongue!'

Strong words that may lead us to ask the Lord for the strength always to speak well of others, and thus contribute very positively to harmony in our staff.

Co-operation

In Strine, a humorous transcription of the way Australians are said to talk, one of the terms is 'aorta', as in the saying 'aorta [they ought to] do something about that'.

'They' refers to all of those powers – in government, Church, school, etc. – that preside over us.

As we stand in the classroom, we may be aware of the identity of some of these powers: our Principal, Deputy Principal, bureaucrats, and so on. Others will be unknown to us, but we are aware that they formulate policies and regulations, some of which we find difficult to cope with and so we say 'Aorta do something about that'.

Our leaders, especially our school leaders, are at the interface between the school and the public; consequently, they are subject to pressures, some of which they must keep to themselves, and many of which cause much anxiety. In their sometimes lonely position, they need wisdom and strength to work for the common good.

We owe our leaders loyalty and respect.

Co-operation

> Nor ever repeat gossip to the betraying of another's secret. If of such things you are ashamed, shame shall you never feel, and you shall find favour with everyone.
>
> Sirach 42:1

In class, in our dealings with parents and colleagues, we hear many details about others' lives.

Sometimes, people confide in us; sometimes, facts are just blurted out, while at other times we overhear snippets of conversation that are meant to be private, or we may come across documents that are meant to be confidential.

Often the things we learn are natural secrets: matters which of their very nature we are bound to keep to ourselves, or, on rare occasions, reveal only to competent authorities.

Nobody pretends that keeping secrets is easy. We itch to relate what we have learned, particularly if it smacks of the sensational.

We might reflect on the way we treat confidential information, being grateful for those who have respected our confidences, and hoping for the strength and discretion to protect others' reputations.

Co-operation

> This is a devilish place for factions.

This was the impression taken away by an early visitor to a certain locality.

Schools have many functional groupings: primary/secondary; infants/senior primary; middle school/senior school; special needs/mainstream; subject area/ subject area...

Normally, we find support from, and socialise with, colleagues in the group in which we work.

It is not unknown for groups to be at war with each other: personality clashes; inequitable distribution of resources; space; change in status – these are some of the causes.

Factionalism can erode the unity of a staff and make working life a misery.

We support unity in our staff, regretting any disunity we may have caused, and being grateful for the peacemakers among us.

Co-operation

> I swear... to reckon him who taught me this art equally dear to me as my parents, to share my substance with him, and relieve his necessities as required...
> From the *Hippocratic Oath*, c. 400 BC

This famous oath spells out the ethics that physicians promised to observe; the article cited above touches on professional loyalty and solidarity.

We are told that teachers in seventeenth-century France expressed this solidarity by calling each other 'brother'.

While we do not continue this part of the tradition, we still respect professional loyalty.

At times, it is carried to extremes when people interpret it as requiring a cover up or collusion. As John F. Kennedy remarked, we have to get along without going along.

When teachers criticise colleagues to students or parents, professional solidarity goes out the window.

As in all other fields of human activity, the Christian vision is meant to enrich what is already good. Affection for others is good; St Paul advises us to outdo each other in showing honour to each other. Jesus declared that love for each other was the mark by which his disciples would be recognised.

We thank God for the support of our colleagues, and asking for the strength to practise loyalty and charity to them all.

Co-operation

> And Joshua did battle as Moses bade him, going out to do battle with Amalec, while Moses, Aaron and Hur went up to the hill top. Whenever Moses lifted his hands, Israel had the better of it; only when he rested a little did the victory go to Amalec. But now Moses' arms grew weary: so they found him a stone to sit on and bade him be seated on it: then, one on each side, Aaron and Hur kept his arms lifted up. In this way, the strength of his arms held up until set of sun, while Joshua routed Amalec and all the forces Amalec could rally, at the sword's point.
>
> Exodus 17:10-14

Setting aside the historical aspects of this incident, there are some important principles involved.

As the surrounding verses make clear, the whole enterprise was directed by God, and Moses acted in accordance with his wishes.

In carrying them out, people had a different role: Moses to pray, Aaron and Hur to support him, Joshua to do the fighting. It was obviously important for each to perform the assigned role and not someone else's.

Those who were in the thick of battle may well have thought that the three on the hill top had it easy.

The division of labour in schools can cause discontent. Some members of staff may feel that they have to do all the extras, while others seem scarcely to do even what is prescribed.

People have to consider what is a fair thing for all, and also what – given a person's talents (and limitations) – can reasonably be expected from him or her.

It is unlikely that a perfect balance will ever be struck.

We need generosity to do our fair share of the work, and also for patience when arrangements do not seem entirely fair.

Co-operation

> Jesus burst into tears and the Jews remarked: 'Look how dearly he loved him'.
>
> John 11:35-36

Jesus had come to the grave of his friend, Lazarus, and was deeply affected.

Bereavements occur in schools.

Schools are places for the young, who have their whole lives before them. Sadly, some children die through accident, illness or suicide.

We weep.

We grieve when a parent dies, leaving a family desolate. We mourn when a colleague, or former colleague, dies.

We might pray for deceased students, parents and colleagues and for those who struggle to come to terms with their grief

Co-operation

> ... stand firm and hold the traditions which you have learned...
>
> 2 Thessalonians 2:14

Many schools were founded by members of Religious Orders. There may no longer be any Religious in a particular school, but most Orders have taken steps to see that their traditions live on the school.

By traditions, we understand the values and vision (often called 'charism') that inspired the Religious, and to some extent, some of the customs and practices that imparted a special character to schools conducted by the Order.

By trying to put the values and vision into practice and by keeping up the customs, we remain in association with the members of the Order and with their work.

In the dimension of ecclesial communion, there is a growing awareness in every consecrated person of the great cultural and pedagogical wealth that derives from sharing a common educational mission, even in the specificity of the various ministries and charisms.

Consecrated Persons and their Mission in Schools, para 82

If the Religious are to share in the way envisaged by the Congregation for Catholic Education, they need to be invited, to feel that their contributions are welcome.

We esteem the work of the Religious who preceded us, and seek a deeper understanding of the traditions we have received.

Co-operation

> Behold how good and pleasant it is for brethren to dwell together in unity.
>
> Psalm 133:1

Students are accurate observers of the way teachers interact with each other: they know which teachers are close friends and those who are hostile to each other.

Students who witness a harmonious workplace are very well served.

Co-operation

> 'So this is the errand, my friend, on which you have come.'
>
> Matthew 26:50

This is the way Matthew records the way Jesus greeted Judas, who having betrayed him, arrived with an armed guard.

Translators struggle with this greeting. The one constant is 'friend' (though a couple of them opt for 'comrade').

Judas was 'friend', despite turning his back on Jesus and everything they had shared together..

This is a remarkable act of forgiveness.

Perhaps in the course of our career, we have been let down, or even betrayed by a colleague or students whom we trusted.

Perhaps we have let down or betrayed someone who trusted us.

It is a big ask in such circumstances to forgive, or to seek forgiveness, but that is what is required of us.

Co-operation

> Co-operation Productivity, Productivity, Productivity...

The industrialist Henry Ford (1863-1947) introduced his Model T in 1908; eventually, there were over fifteen million on roads throughout the world. By mobilising the assembly line and continually introducing economies, he made the car increasingly affordable.

When he reflected on the workplace, he believed that it was insufficient to hire workers if they were not able to work together.

While some people may consider that Ford's understanding of industrial relations was not always benign, no one can doubt that working together can lead to success.

The bonding that can accompany working together can cheer the soul.

On the other hand, bonding can lead to the exclusion of newcomers and unwillingness to change. The old guard can be a formidable force for preserving professional standards or for professional atrophy.

Our workplace will obviously benefit by working together with open mind and open heart.

Co-operation

> I'm going to try to repeat this [theme] a number of times... gradually increasing the orchestra.
> Maurice Ravel (1875-1837) on the origin of *Bolero* (1928)

Maurice Ravel's most well-known composition is probably the haunting orchestral work, *Bolero*.

Even those of us who are not musical specialists cannot fail to be impressed by the skill of the instrumentalists as, one by one, they each begin to contribute to the theme.

The work begins with the drummer who plays 120 beats per minute throughout the work. He is first joined by the flute, then the clarinet, the strings, brass and so on.

A video performance of *Bolero* is often played in conferences where the purpose is to foster team work: musicians each use their instruments to contribute to the collective endeavour.

The video has been used to good effect in schools.

6

On mindfulness: being centred

> ... mindful of the words spoken before by holy prophets...
>
> 2 Peter 3:12

The prophets testified 'in fragmented and varied fashion' (Hebrews 1:1) to God's presence in the history of his chosen people. Israelites were enjoined to be ever mindful of this presence and to take practical steps to remember it. For example, they were required to place a mezuzah (a parchment containing key biblical quotations and enclosed in a wood or metal container) on their door posts; it was to be touched with reverence on each entrance and departure.

While Christians do not share this practice, we believe that 'in him we live and move and have our being' (Acts 17:28) that is, that God is always present to us.

Events like illness, bereavement, stress or danger may make us strongly mindful of God's presence; then, and in our daily prayer, we try to address the God who goes with us.

Our mindfulness of God's presence may be challenged by life's hustle and bustle, our leisure activities or our lot in life.

Jesus told his followers – ordinary people like us, dealing with life's highs and lows – that they should 'always pray and not give up'.

In our ministry in Catholic schools, we obviously need to be mindful of God's presence as we go about the work he has given us.

'Mindfulness' is a term that is here taken to mean consciousness of God's presence and our dependence on him on the one hand and, on the other, our response to him. In short, prayerfulness.

Mindfulness

> O God, if there be a God, help me, if you can.
> An agnostic's prayer.

We may feel that we have to wait until we are holy enough before we begin to speak to God. We may feel like the character in one of Somerset Maugham's novels who believed that when he met God, both of them were going to feel embarrassed.

All we can do is begin from where we are, not from where we would (or should) like to be. It is helpful to remember the story of the Pharisee and the publican (Luke 18:9-14): the publican was possibly something of a stand-over merchant, but in humbly admitting the truth about himself before God, he found favour with him.

Sometimes the agnostic's prayer may be a starting point for our prayer.

Mindfulness

> My God, if you exist make me know you.
> Charles de Foucauld (1858-1916)

Born into the aristocracy and wealth, blessed with a keen intelligence, de Foucauld graduated from Saint Cyr, the French military academy, and was posted to French Algeria. He left the army to devote himself to the study of native languages and the terrain. For his research and publications, he was awarded a prestigious prize.

In his youth, he had abandoned belief in religion and religious practices. He led a life of debauchery. His parents were dead but he had many close relatives who treated him with love and tolerance. He found himself moved by the example of their lived Christianity, and began to say the prayer quoted above.

One day in 1886, he felt himself drawn to the Church of St Augustin in Paris. It was there in a place now marked by a plaque that he found himself reconciled to the God whose existence he had doubted.

After many false starts, he settled as a hermit in Tamanrasset among the Tuareg whom he considered his family. In fact, he believed that he was a brother to everyone.

It all began with him saying a prayer while doubting whether anyone was listening.

Mindfulness

> Called or uncalled, God is always there.

The Swiss psychiatrist Carl Jung (1875-1961) made this quotation his own.

He found it in the writings of a sixteenth-century theologian, Erasmus, who, in turn, claimed to have found it in ancient Greek texts.

Jung mounted the text over the entrance to the Tower where he withdrew to reflect. Perhaps in spirit we might do the same for our classrooms.

Mindfulness

> Admirable in design and execution

The poet John Berryman (1914-1972) began life as a devout altar boy but, later, his life took many a tortuous twist. It was frequently described as 'turbulent': he inflicted much suffering on himself and those close to him. Towards the end of his life, he revisited the faith of his youth, but in an intensely personal way: he admired the architect who designed the snowflake, he was a compelling author and he was grateful that the Father was good to him.

Prayer from the heart in a personal idiom.

Mindfulness

> Blotted out forever be the day of my birth; that night too which gave word that a human life had been conceived in the womb...
> Had but the womb been the tomb for me, had I died at birth, had no lap ever cherished me, no breast ever suckled me, all would be rest now, all would be silence...
> Such people as I that must tread blindfold in a maze of God's making! Even as I sit down to eat the sighs come, grief floods over me unrestrained.
> Job 3:3,11-13, 23

Job didn't hold back when he made these words of Jeremiah his own.

In this wonderful meditation on the mystery of suffering, Job finally finds some of his questions answered and comes to be at peace with God.

But he begins with his pain, his doubts, his anger, all of which he describes to the best of his ability, and from the heart.

In his agony in the garden, Jesus' heart was ready to break with sorrow and that was the starting point for his prayer at that time.

Mindfulness

> Long distance... person to person...

Some of us will remember that before mobiles and WhatsApp, phone calls interstate or overseas had to be arranged with the government (PMG) switchboard. Costs were calculated according to the duration of the call which was often limited to three minutes. To ensure that our long-distance call could be used to best advantage, we could inform the switchboard that we wanted to make our call 'person to person'.

To our students, prayer may often seem to them a long distance call at best. They need help to experience prayer person to person. Hopefully we can speak from our own experience,

Mindfulness

> In the name of the Father and of the Son and of the Holy Spirit. Amen.

The tracing of a small cross on the forehead seems to have been a common practice among Christians at least by the year 200. The current practice of tracing the larger cross upon ourselves seems to have been in use for the best part of 1000 years.

As we trace the cross, we invoke the Trinity.

Although we cannot plumb the depths of this mystery, when we make the sign of the cross with our students, we have the opportunity to anchor ourselves in the presence of the Trinity dwelling within us.

Mindfulness

> O Lord, thou knowest how busy I must be this day; if I forget thee, do not thou forget me.
>
> Jacob Astley (1579-1652)

Astley was the commander of Charles I's foot soldiers at the Battle of Edgehill in 1642. This, the first battle of the Civil War, ended with both sides claiming victory, with both sides losing about 1500 men. Obviously, Astley would have had much on his mind.

It is an understatement to say that teachers are busy people. After completing arrangements at home, fighting through traffic, dealing with notices, learning of the loss of a 'free' period because of a colleague's absence, waiting in the queue at the photocopier etc. etc., the teacher begins the day in class.

We are told that sometimes Jesus and the disciples were so busy that they didn't have time to eat. It was after such times that Jesus would move away to ground himself in prayer.

We might pray that we do not become so habitually immersed in detail that we lose contact with the Lord, who is always with us, keeping us in mind.

Mindfulness

> My presence, the Lord said, shall go before you, and bring you to your resting place.
>
> Exodus 33:13-14

We are told that Moses spoke to God face-to-face. The cloud by day and the pillar of fire by night assured the people of Israel that God was with them

Such privileges are not granted to us.

Nevertheless, faith tells us that God is always close to us. As the Sufis put it, God is closer to us than our jugular vein.

Opportunities for prolonged prayer are hard to come by, but frequent, momentary, reminders that God is lovingly with us are possible for us all.

Mindfulness

> We speak as Christ would have us speak in the presence of God.
>
> 2 Corinthians 12:19

It is a privilege to be called to spread the news that God is lovingly present in the world and in the lives of every person.

It is also a privilege to spread the news that God the Son entered human history, shaped it according to his plan – mysterious as it is – and now is ever living to intercede for us.

When we try to spread this news in class, whether explicitly during an RE lesson, or implicitly by the way we go about our tasks, we can be certain that God is there with us, acting as he sees fit: however, what he sees as being fit does not always correspond with our view, or our sense of timing. As Teilhard de Chardin pointed out, we become impatient with process and chafe to see the ending.

We thank God for the privilege of working with him, and ask for the grace to speak in his presence as he would have us speak.

Mindfulness

> ... but I have prayed for you that your faith may not fail; when, after a while you have come back to me, it is for you to be the support of your brothers.
>
> Luke 22:32

Jesus prayed for Peter and for the other apostles.

We can follow his example by taking our home room list and speaking to the Lord of the needs of our students, as we understand them.

Mindfulness

> The time of business does not differ with me from the time of prayer; and in the noise and clutter of my kitchen, while several persons are at the same time calling for different things, I possess God in as great tranquility as if I were upon my knees at the Blessed Sacrament.
>
> Br Lawrence (died 1691)

Brother Lawrence was a French Carmelite lay brother. His days were spent in the kitchen or mending sandals. People who were inspired by his words and example collected his letters. They were published in a little booklet entitled The Practice of the Presence of God. It is still available and may be downloaded from the internet.

We learn that his attention to the presence of God required great effort. But this presence, as Cardinal Newman was to say, is 'heart-rending, heart-changing, ever accessible and open to penetration'.

We might pray for a greater awareness of the presence of God in the noise and clutter of our classroom.

Mindfulness

> There is only one point in the universe where God communicates with us and that is in the centre of our own soul.
>
> William Bernard Ullathorne (1806-1889)

Few people have had such a distinguished, selfless, career in Church and state as Ullathorne.

Sent in his mid-twenties to take charge of the Church in Australia, he showed a cool head in dealing with difficult people and sectarian bitterness. He strongly opposed the transportation of convicts to Australia.

Having returned to England, he was eventually consecrated Bishop of Birmingham. His judgment, tact and sense of purpose helped him to contribute to the re-establishment of a Catholic hierarchy in England and to moderate disputes at the First Vatican Council.

A scholarly man, he was also a man of prayer.

In the midst of the turmoil in which he frequently found himself, he found counsel and support in God's presence, as he said, in the centre of his own soul.

We encourage our students to be aware of God's presence in the centre of their soul.

Mindfulness

> The Eucharistic Sacrifice is the source and summit of the Christian life.
> Vatican II, *Dogmatic Constitution on the Church*, Ch 2.

No matter how intense our prayers, we must recognise that the Mass is **the** prayer.

We work towards an increased awareness of the reality in which participate at Mass, and a greater devotion to it.

Mindfulness

> Children become ever more aware of the gift of faith they have received and they learn in addition to worship God the Father in spirit and in truth, especially in liturgical action.
> Vatican II, *Declaration on Christian Education*, Ch 2.

It is no secret that surveys show that many children find the Mass 'boring', As teachers who take children to Mass, we don't need surveys to tell us that.

Apart from the tragedy of being indifferent, or even hostile, to the Mass, students can suffer from a loss of the sense of the sacred.

Guidelines and many books have been published dealing with children's liturgies, and, as classroom teachers, we must rely on the guidance of the experts.

We are called to work with the priest, our colleagues and the children themselves to make the Mass as meaningful for them as we can.

We need guidance and success in this work, which is central to Catholic life.

Mindfulness

True Catholic prayer will always include devotion to Mary the Mother of God: God himself gave her this pre-eminent role and endowed her with the gifts of nature and grace to fulfil it.

In the words 'Mother, this is your son' and 'This is your mother', Jesus was not only ensuring that Mary would have someone to look after her when he was gone: Christians have seen in this exchange the announcement of the special role that Mary was to play in the life of the Church, in the life of all Christians.

Moreover, Mary was the first teacher of Jesus: she is thus a special model for us.

We might pray for Our Lady's help, now and at the hour of our death.

Mindfulness

If we consider Our Lady as she is presented in the Gospels, we find her seeking for understanding: 'How can this be?'. 'Child, why did you behave towards us in this way? Oh, our hearts were heavy – your father's and mine – as we searched for you.'

Or we find her in puzzling situations: hearing the prophecy of Simeon that her soul would be pierced with a sword; her quest with others of Jesus' relatives, early in his ministry, to find out just what he was doing; standing by when her son was executed. Jesus asked, 'Why?' With a mother's love, how forcefully she would have asked that question!

St Luke tells us that 'his mother treasured all these [infancy] incidents in her memory'.

Mary's search is our model for a faith that seeks understanding.

We might pray to Our Lady asking for a right understanding of our vocation and a deeper understanding of her son.

Mindfulness

In Dura-Europos, a site in eastern Syria above the Euphrates, are the remains of what is thought to be one of the earliest Christian churches.

On the wall, there is a painting of a woman drawing water from a well. It has been interpreted as depicting the Annunciation.

Mary is thus shown to be busy helping her family. In early Christian thought, Our Lady was revered as Mother of God and Helper.

Our Lady's role as helper is the theme of the 'Sub tuum praesidium', perhaps the earliest prayer addressed to her. Our students will benefit from learning it.

> We fly to thy protection,
> O holy Mother of God.
> Despise not our petitions in our necessities,
> but deliver us always from all dangers,
> O glorious and blessed Virgin.

Mindfulness

> Glory be to the Father and to the Son and to the Holy Spirit.
> As it was in the beginning, is now, and ever shall be, world without end. Amen.

This short hymn of praise and faith in the Trinity has been in use since the 600s.

While it is still used in the Divine Office and in the Rosary, it may not be well known to a number of students.

It is a prayer whose length will not weary and whose meaning is profound.

It is another way in which we can anchor ourselves and our students in the presence of God and in our fundamental beliefs.

Mindfulness

> Jesus answered: 'Were not ten made clean? And the other nine, where are they? Not one has come back to give God the praise except this stranger'.
>
> Luke 17:17-18.

An old hymn used to run:

Count your blessings
Count them one by one
And it will surprise you
What the Lord has done.

The hymn was a reminder to give thanks for all the good things we have received.

Jesus was surprised that people cured of leprosy would not return to show gratitude.

It is possible to pray only to ask for things; it is easy to forget to give thanks.

Mindfulness

> ... just as day was breaking, Jesus stood on the beach... When Simon Peter learned it was the Master.. he plunged into the lake. When they had come ashore they noticed hot embers on the ground, with fish lying on the fire and bread.
>
> John 21:4, 7, 9

Seemingly at a loose end, Peter had decided to go fishing. Other disciples joined him. They caught nothing. In the midst of their failure, Jesus called to them. In spite of his betrayal, Peter immediately jumped into the lake and swam to Jesus, who met Peter's immediate need by providing breakfast. It was only then that he helped Peter to repent of his denials.

We need to share with our students our assurance that no matter what people may have done, the risen Jesus will always call to them and welcome their return to him.

7

On teaching: teaching and learning

> Jesus began to do and to teach.
>
> Acts 1:1

Teaching is the setting of our faith, vocation, collegiality, dedication and prayer.

Doing and teaching are our privilege and our duty.

Teaching

> School days, school days
> Dear old golden rule days
> Readin' and 'ritin' and 'rithmetic.
> Taught to the tune of a hick'ry stick...
>
> 'School Days', Will D. Cobb & Gus Edwards, (1907)

Such was the curriculum and such was the mode of classroom management in perhaps less complicated times.

However, there is continuity in that, then and now, teachers are concerned with literacy, numeracy and the transmission of values.

While these days, literacy and numeracy are interpreted more broadly, approaches to classroom management are more varied and values are often contested, it is not unreasonable humbly to assert the value of teaching; and it is perhaps not too fanciful to suggest that teaching remains the midwife of all other professions.

Teaching

> Post-Christian, a-political, uncultivated, with no feeling for the past...

This is how a young teacher described the milieu of his first school.

In appearance, it was like a shoebox set among stunted shrubs, without anything to catch the eye or stimulate interest. Anyway, the students were not interested and didn't want to be interested.

Teachers despaired when they crossed the threshold, feeling they were ploughing water which immediately closed over their efforts.

When he was allocated Year 9 classes, he felt he had been 'dumped in the shit'.

It became a matter of eighteen hours a week and then escape back to town.

It would be great if the school thus described was a figment of the imagination. Sadly, it is only too real

A dynamic vision and sustained concerted efforts, mutual support and the support of the school administration are needed to manage individuals or classes or cohorts or schools which show a complete lack of interest in what we need to teach.

Teaching

> Then Jesus, accompanied by his disciples, withdrew toward the sea and a large mass of people followed...
> Mark 3:7
>
> I hate the common masses and avoid them.
> Horace (65-27BC) *Odes*, Book 3

Translators of Mark select 'crowd,' 'multitude,' or, in this case, 'mass'.

The character speaking through the Latin poet Horace may have had in mind people lacking a sense of the sacred, but the statement is often interpreted as a condemnation of the 'hoi polloi', or 'the great unwashed', or 'the rabble', or 'the mob', or undesirables... deplorables ... among any number of other derogatory terms.

In the early days in Australia, while some Catholic schools were established to support the gifted or the significantly impaired, most catered for the masses, who left school as soon as they were entitled to enter the workforce. It is only in the last fifty years or so that tertiary education has been a realistic aspiration for more than a minority.

These days, some people enrol their children in a Catholic school, not because it's Catholic but because it is 'private'. They are welcome.

However, perhaps not unfairly, some in the government school sector maintain that private schools, including Catholic schools, pick and choose and exclude, leaving teachers in State Schools to teach the masses.

Teaching

> With every kindly sympathy and affection blasted in its birth, with every young and healthy feeling flogged and starved down, with every revengeful passion that can fester in swollen heart eating its evil way to their core in silence, what an incipient Hell was breeding here.
>
> Charles Dickens, Nicholas Nickleby, 1838

Nicholas has found employment as a teacher in Dotheboys Hall, a school conducted by Mr Wackford Squeers and his wife. A visitor's surprise at first meeting Mr Squeers, with his one eye and unkempt appearance, was intensified by the sight of Mrs Squeers ladling generous spoonfuls of treacle and brimstone into children's mouths. This measure, together with starvation and flogging, were their main educational and managerial techniques.

The quotation records Nicholas' realisation when he first laid eyes on his pupils: the effects of the Squeers' pedagogy were laid bare.

He was moved to try and make things better.

Teaching

> 'He taught us good.'

This is the way in which an elderly sporting hero recalled one of his teachers from long ago.

Evidently, the teacher's specialty was not English grammar, but something far more important: the ability to touch the heart of his student, to teach him what was important for him at that stage of his life and to make him feel that his talents were worthwhile.

Most people can remember at least one teacher who influenced them in the same way.

They accept what the teacher stood for and have internalised the teacher's values. Long after the lesson content has been forgotten, the values live on.

Teaching

> Delight

John Francis Whelan (1900-1991) adopted the pen name of Seán Ó'Faoláin, and attained distinction as a writer in Ireland.

He recalled his days in an elementary school conducted by the Presentation Brothers in Cork.

In particular, he remembered the last few days before the long holidays when the Brothers allowed some latitude and the little boys listened with delight to the wind blowing under the door. They would roll their eyes and say 'Ooh!'

His words remind us that young children the world over are blessed with exuberance, laughter and delight.

Their introduction to the Christian message should do nothing but enhance these qualities.

Teaching

> The thrill of creation

André Malraux (1901-1976) was a French novelist and theoretician of the arts.

He believed that when we look at a work of art, we share to some extent in the creative impulse of the artist.

While teaching is not a graphic art, it is certainly a craft. There are very many teachers who, often in difficult circumstances, excel in the exercise of their craft.

We rejoice as we acknowledge the diversity of the outstanding achievements of our colleagues.

Teaching

> Let us now praise famous people that were our ancestors long ago...
>
> Sirach 44:1

Written around 200 BC in the Middle East, this book of the Bible reflects the social hierarchy of its time of composition.

Let us now praise great educators, women and men, who have gone before us.

Among these, we can recall Anne Sullivan (1866-1936).

Afflicted at an early age with trachoma and thus partially blind, she was abandoned by her father and committed to an institution. Despite her disability and the abuses practised in the institution, she managed to be transferred to a school for the blind and made rapid progress in acquiring the techniques of teaching those with this disability.

At the age of 20, she was appointed tutor to Helen Keller, who had been struck blind and deaf at the age of nineteen months. Sullivan adapted the techniques she had been taught, and mentored Keller, who went on to achieve academic honours and fame as a writer and lecturer. Sullivan remained her life-long companion.

Anne Sullivan was an outstanding educator.

In a speech delivered when she graduated from her training course, she observed

> ... every success we achieve tends to bring people closer to God and make life more as he would have it.

Teaching

> *Ordinary People, Extraordinary Teachers: The Heroes of Real India.*

This is the title of a book written by S. Giridhar, the Chief Operating Officer of Azim Preji University in Bengaluru (formerly Bangalore), in the Indian State of Karnataka (Mysore).

He claims to have studied teachers at work in government schools throughout India, and to have been impressed by their innovation, creativity, resourcefulness and tenacity as well as by their strict but humane management of classes.

He regards them as heroes.

The qualities that impressed him are also exhibited by so many of our colleagues – ordinary people who are extraordinary teachers.

Teaching

> Many daughters have done well, but you excel them all.
>
> Proverbs 31:29

It is one of the joys of teaching to see girls and boys excel.

Schools proudly list their former students who have achieved distinction.

It is a special source of satisfaction when some of them attribute their achievements to us personally.

It is also a source of satisfaction to acknowledge the many alumni who, while not recognised as distinguished, are constructive members of the community.

We thank God for our successes.

Teaching

> Marcel Marceau, French Resistance fighter and mime artist

Marcel Marceau (1923-2007) was a mime artist who had the good fortune to recognise his special gift and to develop it. He performed with acclaim in many countries for 60 years.

When Marceau died, the journalist Jacques Chancel observed that in silence he had said more than many people who speak at length.

Each of us has a brace of strengths, which form the basis of our teaching style. They help us to feel comfortable in our teaching skin.

They help us to communicate with students who are on our wavelength.

It is a sobering fact that not all students will be on our wavelength. We may teach them content, but they will not resonate with us. We need to accept this limitation.

We seek to understand how our gifts can be used to good purpose in the classroom.

Teaching

> It was by many such parables that he announced the message in a manner suited to their capacity.
> Mark 4:33

The way in which Jesus dealt with two bereavements illustrates how he varied his strategy to suit the people involved.

When he restored to life the only son of the widow of Naim, he was dealing with a woman who was now totally alone. No doubt grief and the hopelessness of her situation put her beyond discussion and instruction.

> The sight of her touched the Lord's heart, and he said to her: 'Do not weep'.
> He then went up to the coffin and laid his hand on it. The bearers stopped and he said: 'Young man, I command you, awake!' The dead man sat up and began to speak. He then restored him to his mother.
> Luke 7:13-15.

The raising of Lazarus (John 11:1-48.) is much more elaborate. The miracle entailed the instruction of Martha, Mary, the apostles and the onlookers generally:

> 'Father, I thank you for listening to me. For myself, I knew that you always hear me; but I said it for the sake of the people surrounding me, that they might believe that I am your ambassador.'

We know that it is very rare to have a class of uniform ability; certainly, we will never have a class where every student's temperament and personal needs are identical.

We may pride ourselves in treating students equally, but we know that we cannot treat each of them in the same way.

Unfortunately, we are not infallible: our strategies will not always be suitable. We will not always have the patience and wisdom to do and say exactly what each child needs.

But we can aspire to this success.

Teaching

> How then shall I characterise the people of this generation? Of whom do they remind me? They remind me of little children sitting about the market place and calling out to their partners:
>
> > 'We played you a tune to make you merry,
> > and yet you did not dance:
> > we played you a tune to make you sorry,
> > and yet you did not strike your breasts'.
>
> Luke 7:32

What a great feeling it is when we click with a class. It is a joy to teacher and student alike.

How heart-breaking it is when we just cannot get along with a class, no matter what we try. We think we just can't win.

These contrasting situations can occur from one year to the next, or in the same year if we teach parallel classes. The content and method may be the same, but the interaction is so different.

Jesus was confronted with the same situation.

We are grateful for our successes, and hope for courage, patience and sweetness of temper when things go painfully wrong.

Teaching

> There is no credit in spending all your time on the cream of your pupils. Try rather to bring the more troublesome ones to order, by using gentleness. Nobody can heal every wound with the same ointment.
> From a letter of Ignatius of Antioch to Polycarp.

Here we are almost back at the beginning: Polycarp was a disciple of St John, so we are looking at a letter written around 100 AD.

In some respects, not much has changed since then. It is still easy to concentrate on the cream of our students rather than on the difficult ones.

The impact of such conduct on pupils can affect the rest of their school lives. For example, an alienated Year 10 student recalled quite clearly when he realised that school was not for him. It was in Year 1. His teacher said to him; 'You're a dum dum. Go down the back and play with the blocks while the rest of us do our sums'.

On the other hand, lavishing so much attention on a pupil that he or she is recognised as a 'teacher's pet' is of no help to the child or the teacher.

We strive for the ability to be even-handed in our dealings with our students and not to shy away from the more difficult ones.

Teaching

> Father Pat Keating SJ – a well-rounded man

Christopher Brennan (1870-1932) was an Australian poet and scholar. In his *Curriculum Vitae*, he dwelt admiringly on the skills and learning of his teacher Father Pat Keating SJ.

In particular, Brennan noted Keating's skill in classroom interaction.

Interaction lies at the heart of our work as teachers. To some extent it is dictated by circumstances: location; type of lesson; age and qualities of our students, our temperament...

It also depends on our personal style and our relationship with students.

It is important that we adopt the strategies that will help students to learn stipulated content. As Brennan's experience shows, in such learning experiences we teach a lot more besides.

Teaching

> My object all sublime
> I shall achieve in time
> To let the punishment fit the crime
> The punishment fit the crime...
>
> W. S. Gilbert, *The Mikado*

The song goes on to make fun of various social failings, but fitting the punishment or correction to the crime is, of course, no laughing matter.

People may recall reading, or seeing the film of, Herman Wouk's novel, *The Caine Mutiny*. One episode depicts the neurotic captain delivering a very lengthy reprimand to a seaman for a minor infraction. In the process, the captain loses all sense of the action in which his ship is involved.

Unless our delivery is always spellbinding, we will at times be obliged to recall to the task a student whose attention has strayed. It requires no little skill to do so consistently without alienating the student (and the class) and without losing the thread of the lesson. Sarcasm and anger can undermine interaction.

We need lightness of touch to ensure that our corrections really do fit the crime.

Teaching

> *ancilla*. n., maid-servant.

The English adjective 'ancillary' is derived from the above Latin word.

It is sometimes used to denote staff who act as secretaries, clerks, receptionists, security officers, support staff in laboratories and libraries, janitors...

These members of staff provide services without which a school would collapse.

Engaged with the reality of students' lives outside the classroom, they often see and hear things of which teachers and administration may be unaware. (They may also witness the unscheduled entries, exits and other errant behaviour of some teaching staff.)

We esteem and are very grateful for the service and discretion of our 'ancillary' colleagues; we regret any time when we have overlooked all that they do for us or when we have not accorded them the respect they deserve.

Teaching

> Look at this: a sower went out to plant seed. While he was sowing, some fell along a path, and the birds flew down and ate it up. Some also fell on rocky ground where the soil was very poor; it sprouted very quickly, since the soil was not very deep. But when the sun came up, the sprouts were scorched; and since they had no root, they quickly dried up. Other seeds landed among the thornbushes...
>
> Mark 4:3-7

Mark tells us that Jesus was 'teaching in town after town and village after village'. (It is estimated that there were 200 such settlements in Galilee at that time.) It is likely that he used this parable many times, and the early Christians would have told it over and over until it was written down.

Words may have been changed here and there but the basic structure and purpose remain.

Jesus observed the range of reactions to his message and discerned a pattern. Further, he was able to express his understanding through concrete comparisons.

According to scholars, the interpretation of the parable (verses 11-20) is the response of the early Church as it reflected on Jesus' words. He was a teacher who engaged his disciples to construct their understanding of the lesson he had taught them.

At times, we may have been swept along by a sudden inspiration, but we all realise that there is no substitute for reflection on what we are to teach and careful preparation of our lessons.

What one writer calls a 'sense of craft' compels us to look upon 'winging it' as unworthy of us. The same can be said of merely churning out the same thing year after year; this is a mind-numbing experience for teacher and student alike.

Teaching

> A preacher who does not prepare is not 'spiritual'; he is dishonest and irresponsible with the gifts he has received.
>
> Pope Francis, *Evangelii Gaudium*, para. 145

The Pope here is commenting on those preachers who maintain that they have so much to do that they do not have the time to devote to the lengthy preparation of their homilies.

As we know, teaching is not preaching: sermons in the classroom are doomed to failure.

While teachers are not preachers, adequate preparation is an indispensable component of the craft of teaching.

Teaching

> 1,1,2,3,5,8,13,21,34,55...

This set of numbers is known as the Fibonacci Sequence, after the mathematician who wrote a treatise on it around the year 1200. The sequence is capable of sophisticated development.

Most of us will not be dealing with this pattern in class, but no matter what we teach, we try to lead our students to see what they are learning as part of a coherent pattern.

Moreover, the pattern we present must be true.

In days gone by, a textbook used in Catholic schools explained the Reformation as the result of the greed of German princes. No doubt the writer wanted to present the Church in the best light, but we realise that the causes of the Reformation were far more complex.

Arriving at a balanced understanding is one of our professional obligations – part of our preparation for our work with our students.

It's not always easy – as the poet said, 'knowledge hath a bloody entry'.

Teaching

> ... once in Crete the legendary labyrinthine passages wound through darkened walls and countless paths that muddled every clue.
>
> Virgil, *Aeneid*, Book V

According to the myth, the labyrinth had been constructed to contain the Minotaur, a monster, half-bull and half-human, which used to devour hostages offered to it. The mythical hero, Theseus, found his way through the labyrinth, slew the Minotaur, and with help of the beautiful Ariadne, managed to find his way out again.

Perhaps, we can recall being obliged to study a subject or a topic which was as puzzling as the labyrinth. Maybe we were defeated or blundered through by rote and short cuts, without ever really understanding subject matter or intent; we may have passed, but knew that we shouldn't have. Or, we may have been fortunate enough to have a guide who helped us to find a point of engagement and then to progress.

We know only too well that many of our students are reluctant to be led into a new topic; others become completely lost in the labyrinth.

Sadly, Theseus abandoned Ariadne. Students are not always grateful for our guidance, but we offer it just the same.

Teaching

> Nobody was able to answer him a word; from that day forward, no one dared to ask him any more questions.
>
> Matthew 22:46

There were many occasions when authorities sprang questions on Jesus to trip him up. He was always more than equal to the challenge confronting him.

In such circumstances, Jesus did not have the chance to prepare his answer: he had to speak from his convictions. As he commented: 'The mouth speaks out of the abundance of the heart' (Luke 6:25).

No matter how well we are prepared, there are times in class when we are tripped up.

Sometimes, students, aware that we are not masters of a topic or a subject generally, may take pleasure in exposing our ignorance.

At other times, despite our expertise, there will be questions we cannot answer on the spot.

We may bluster or become angry: neither approach helps the students or us. Punishments imposed to prop up our authority are invariably counter-productive.

These are times when we must draw upon our reserves of honesty and good humour.

Teaching

General Sir John Monash (1865-1931) has been described as one of the most outstanding generals on the Western Front in World War I.

Far from looking upon his troops as cannon fodder, he did everything he could to protect them.

The secret of his success was meticulous planning.

For example, at the battle of Hamel (July 1918), he calculated that, by employing an integrated use of weaponry, troops would secure their primary objective in 90 minutes: in fact, it took 93 minutes. The troops were amazed that his planning included the provision of hot meals for them at the front.

We aspire to a similar sense of professionalism

Teaching

> Some people have failed to hit the mark, and have turned to vain babbling. They crave to be teachers of the Law, when they understand neither what they say nor the points on which they put such stress.
>
> 1 Timothy 1:6-7

As teachers, we have a captive audience – even if they are not always attentive.

It is a matter for thanksgiving that, in this country, teachers are free to choose the political party they prefer, to adopt their own view about the ordering of society and to follow their conscience.

However, as parents, we do not send our children to school to learn their teachers' political views, or their social preferences or their private interpretations of the teachings of the Church.

Yet, it is not unknown for some teachers to seek to influence their captive audience to adopt their interpretations and tastes.

We might justly say that teachers acting in this way have failed to hit the mark.

Teaching

> She awakened an ability to think for ourselves, to 'interpret' as well as comprehend.

This is the way one of the students of Margaret Moses (1940-1975) remembered her.

Margaret Moses began her teaching career as a Nun.

Afterwards, she left the convent and taught in a Technical School. It was here that she so impressed the student quoted above.

Later, Margaret left teaching and went to Vietnam where she helped to look after children orphaned by the war.

As the fall of Saigon became imminent, she boarded a plane to accompany some orphans who were being evacuated. Through a malfunction, the plane crashed, killing her and many of the children.

In various settings, by word and example, Margaret Moses was a passionate teacher.

Teaching

> Who's going to love me now?

One of the many books, Rod Dreher has written is a biography of his sister Ruthie Leming (1969-2011).

She was one of those teachers who have the gift of communicating successfully with a student or group of students who are 'difficult'.

To be honest, many students recall with gratitude some such teachers who succeeded through fear: 'She/he put the fear of God into me'.

Not so, Ruthie. Her warmth and intuitiveness were her main standbys.

Sadly, she died from cancer in the middle of her career.

When she heard that Ruthie had died, one of her more difficult students lamented 'Who's going to love me now?'

An enviable assessment of a teacher's influence.

Teaching

> With the instinct of an unerring marksman, each was constantly on the lookout for the other's weak spot, which once detected became the target for a cloud of poisoned darts.

The French writer Michel Tournier's novel *The Four Wise Men* describes the adventures of the Wise Men who visited the Infant Jesus.

We are accustomed to think of three Wise Men, namely Balthasar, Melchior and Gaspar. Tournier imagines there was a fourth – Taor, Prince of Mangalore.

It was Taor's misfortune always to be just too late, whether to greet the Infant, Mary and Joseph, or to meet Jesus during his ministry.

Taor's travels led him through many perilous adventures and to interesting encounters, one of which was to meet the descendants of survivors in the ruins of Sodom. Among these was a couple whose relationship was described above.

We may encounter colleagues who, having exercised their unerring skill of finding the weak spots of other staff or students, then delight in dwelling upon them.

Some students have this ability. They are bullies.

We pray not to be burdened with such colleagues and for the skill to countermand the bullies.

Teaching

> ... the solitary sobbing of a shepherd's flute burst forth.
> 'What is that?' I asked.
> 'It is Satan weeping as he beholds the beauty of the world.'

A certain king, being trouble by a recent event, took a solitary walk to ponder the matter. He found himself in the presence of an old man going about his tasks and evidently unimpressed by the arrival of royalty. It was in this setting that the king heard the sobbing of the flute and received the old man's reply.

It is a reminder that ranged against beauty. truth and goodness are the Satanic forces, which Jesus spoke of as 'the world'/ Together with the Church at large, our Catholic school seeks to defend and promote beauty, truth and goodness.

Teaching

> Be praised, my Lord, for our sister Mother Earth
> Who feeds and rules us
> And produces various fruits with coloured flowers and herbs.
>
> St Francis of Assisi, *Canticle of the Sun*

St Francis (1181-1226), sometimes described as the person who most resembled Jesus, is revered by people of many religious traditions.

Some admire his simplicity, others his courage, others still, his total devotion to living and preaching the Gospel.

His life and words teach lessons that have retained their force down through the centuries.

Distancing himself from all possessions, he nevertheless treasured creation, what is now called the environment.

Currently, there are disputes about how best to treat the environment.

Schools will be on a sound course if, like St Francis, their teachings and actions demonstrate reverence for the environment as God's creation.

The *Canticle of the Sun* warrants prayerful reflection.

Teaching

> When I was eight and a half, Leonie left the Abbey and I replaced her. I was in a class of older girls and among them was a girl of fourteen, who was not very clever but able to lead the others. She was jealous that, although I was younger, I nearly always topped the class and that I was a favourite with all the nuns, so she found a thousand ways to make me pay for my little achievements. As I was naturally rather shy and sensitive, I did not know how to protect myself. I could only cry and say nothing about it.
>
> St Therese of Lisieux, *The Story of a Soul*.

Therese Martin, as she was then, took her sister's place at a school which was hundreds of years old. She later said that her school years were the unhappiest in her life.

Even saints have experienced bullying!

It is a form of coercion that is practised in schools, workplaces; indeed in most walks of life.

Often the victim can do nothing but cry, inwardly or outwardly.

We may have shed a few tears ourselves in such circumstances.

If, thankfully, we have not ourselves been bullied, we will certainly have seen bullying practised in schools.

Book upon book has been written on the topic and no doubt our school has an anti-bullying policy and there will be staff who can administer specialist care.

As classroom teachers we interact with children indoors and outdoors. As far as in us lies we are called to manage children so that bullying does not occur on our watch.

Teaching

> Those who are engaged in education, especially the education of the young... should regard it as among their greatest responsibilities to educate people to want peace. Every one of us needs a change of heart...
> *Constitution on the Church in the Modern World.*

We rely on world leaders to secure peace. In a democracy, leaders are answerable to their people: consequently, politicians heed citizens' views, if only to be re-elected.

The future citizens of this country are being educated in their homes and in our classrooms.

Interactions in our classrooms are at the heart of our professional activity.

Teachers' words and actions can strongly influence students – for good or ill.

It is important, therefore, that interactions foster peace, leading us all to banish bitterness, vindictiveness and hostility and to see violence as a dangerous delusion – in a word, leading us to a change of heart.

Teaching

> Blessed are the peacemakers...

St Therese of Lisieux had to contend with the nervous mannerisms of another member of her community.

Reflecting on Therese's efforts to avoid irritation, Dorothy Day wrote, 'She began with working for peace in her own heart and willing to love where love was difficult, and so she grew in love and increased the sum total of love in the world, not to speak of peace'.

Students may find this approach helpful.

Teaching

> Heart speaks to heart.
>
> John Henry Newman

This is the motto Newman chose when he was created a Cardinal.

It is a saying that expresses the engagement, the sharing of values, that is the cumulative effect of honest interactions between teacher and taught.

Elsewhere Newman wrote:

> Eloquence or wit, shrewdness or dexterity, these plead a cause well and propagate it quickly, but it dies with them. It has no roots in the heart of others and lives not out a generation.

In other words, a flamboyant approach does more good to the speaker than to the listener.

The faithful and unassuming exercise of our calling, day after day, can create an admirable bond between teacher and taught.

Teaching

> And he told them [the Twelve apostles] to announce the kingdom of God and to heal the sick.
>
> Luke 9:2
>
> He welcomed the crowd and began to speak to them about the kingdom of God and to heal those who needed it.
>
> Luke 9:11

Luke records the duties given to the Twelve when they were sent out on a mission.

On their return, they found Jesus performing the same duties.

Luke obviously intended to demonstrate that the mission of the Twelve was identical to Jesus' own: to announce the kingdom of God and to meet people's pressing needs.

In our ministry of teaching, we are called upon to speak of the kingdom of God. Some ministries still aim to heal the pressing need of illness.

Such is not our calling. We are called respond to other pressing needs of the young: to nurture them, to help them to avoid harmful practices and to acquire learning. Sometimes, our mission also includes making up for shortfalls in their food, clothing and other necessities.

We are thankful for the privilege of sharing in the mission of Jesus.

Teaching

> After this, the Lord appointed seventy-two others and sent them before him...
>
> Luke 10:1

When Jesus sent his disciples on a training mission, he foresaw that it was probable that they would not succeed everywhere: 'Shake off the dust...'

Jesus himself did not succeed everywhere: 'some of his disciples walked no more with him...'

Despite our best efforts, schools do not succeed with every student. Sometimes, it becomes obvious that a continuing association is harmful to the student and the school alike. The student is invited to leave.

There are numerous stories of trivial incidents and minor infractions being used in the past as reasons for asking a student to leave. 'Expulsion, expelled' were the terms usually employed. Sometimes. there was a certain solemnity about the process, like a soldier being drummed out of a regiment.

Those days are gone, if for no other reason than there is always the possibility of litigation. While litigation and other legal concerns must be kept in mind, the prime concern should be the welfare of the student, and that of other students, and staff, whom he or she may have affected.

There will be hurt all round. There will almost certainly be differences of opinion in the school community. Discretion will not always be the most obvious characteristic of discussions.

It falls to the school administration to be guided by truth, justice and charity in bringing the matter to an equitable conclusion.

We hope that our own input will be constructive.

Teaching

> There were others, graceless folk...
> 1 Samuel 10:27

Elsewhere in the Bible, we read of 'scoundrels', 'rabble', or 'worthless fellows'.

Sometimes in schools, there can be difficult groups – apparently 'graceless folk' – that are involved in tussles with the school throughout their stay.

One group may be exuberant and mischievous, with a tincture of malice. Its members may be talented, and individually quite personable, yet in the ensemble there always lurks the possibility of spite. The group will achieve in various fields; one wonders about its members' values.

Another group may be turbulent, with little interest in anything the school has to offer. With the expectation that this group will achieve little, the school may allocate the least able staff to teach them. Students will suffer, staff more so. Experience shows that with a teacher who can communicate with the group and with adjustments to the curriculum – and that does not mean a dumbing down – this group can achieve.

Some students hate school and everything it stands for. Many staff who teach such students suffer acutely.

Unfortunately, there is no magic bullet. We can study success stories and try to apply them to our circumstances.

No student, no teacher, is a worthless fellow, though, on occasion, some may act like one.

In our idealism, it is essential to confront the dreary reality faced by many people – students and teachers – in schools.

We do what we can to make their lives better.

Teaching

> The service of God does not require good words and good desires but efficient workmanship, commitment and courage.
> St Paul of the Cross (1694-1775)

St Paul founded the Passionists. He was a powerful preacher.

At times, we may find it hard to progress from good words and desires to the discipline of systematic engagement in the classroom.

Teaching

A Divinity student was faced with an examination for which he had prepared poorly. He took a gamble and prepared himself to write about the Kings of Israel. When he sat the paper, he found that the question concerned the divinity of Christ. 'When it comes to such a sublime topic', he wrote, 'who am I to write? But when it comes to the Kings of Israel…'

We have all corrected work which is of middling quality at best; perhaps we have been lucky enough to come across a howler or two. The fact remains that grading students' work can be something of a hard slog.

These days, we deal with rubrics, descriptors, benchmarks, outcomes, age-related expected levels of achievements etc., etc. Assessments may be the subject of appeal; accusations of bias may be made; there may be comparisons of the achievements of some teachers and schools…

Nonetheless, the work that we return to students gives us the opportunity to offer supportive and constructive comments – nothing is gained by unkind and belittling observations, no matter how disappointing a student's performance may be.

There can be no doubt that assessment is an integral part of our work with students.

We need patience and wisdom to perform this task well.

Teaching

> It was six men of Indostan
> To learning much inclined
> Who went to see the Elephant
> (Though all of them were blind)
> That each by observation
> Might satisfy his mind.
>
> John Godfrey Saxe (1816-1887)

Saxe retold this story, which appears in many ancient cultures.

The first man comes upon the elephant's flank and declares the animal to be like a wall. The second, feeling the tusk, likens it to a spear. The third, feeling the trunk, likens it to a snake. The next, feeling the elephant's knee, declared it to be like a tree. The fifth, having touched the ear, believed the animal to be like a fan. The last, chancing upon the tail, believed that the elephant was like a rope.

Many of us will have participated in a group activity wherein we all marked the same exercise. We were probably surprised at the range of assessments. Like the learned men of Indostan, we may have interpreted the marking criteria from conflicting perspectives. We may discover that we need to be more flexible – or more demanding.

When we come to an exercise submitted by a student to whom we are not well disposed, we might be tempted to skim over it or to mark it harshly.

Deuteronomy records the instruction that judges should 'dispense true justice to the people' (Deuteronomy 16:18).

Grading and management are areas where true justice is to be dispensed.

Teaching

> He entered the home of the Pharisee and reclined on a couch; and without warning a woman who was a scandal in the town came in. After making sure that he was at table in the home of the Pharisee, she brought with her an alabaster flask of perfume, took her stand behind him at his feet, and wept. Yielding to an impulse, she rained her tears on his feet and wiped them with her hair; she tenderly kissed his feet and anointed them with the perfume.
>
> Matthew 7:36-39

How embarrassed we would be if we found ourselves in this situation!

Such is Jesus' self-possession, so grounded is he in compassion and truth, that he is able to draw out a lesson for his host, and bring healing to the woman: 'Your faith has saved you. Go home and be at peace'.

No matter how well prepared we are, there will always be times when, 'without warning', something is said or done that has the potential to throw us.

Most of us can recall many such occasions, sometimes with amusement, at other times with the realisation that we were wrong footed.

We may have been annoyed that our plans were frustrated; perhaps we felt insulted...

Teaching

> Then out of the district came a Canaanite woman who exclaimed: 'Take pity on me, Master, Son of David! My daughter is sorely tormented by a demon'... He demurred. 'It is not fair,' he said, 'to take the children's bread and throw it to the dogs'. 'You are right, Master', she replied: 'and the dogs eat only of the crumbs that fall from the tables of their masters'. Then Jesus acquiesced. 'My good woman', he said, 'great is your faith! Your wish shall be granted'. Her daughter was cured that very moment.
>
> Matthew 15:22, 26-28

There is no power like a mother's love. Jesus appeared uninterested; the disciples pleaded with him to help her, not from compassion but because they were sick of her pleading. The mother would not take no for an answer, and her wish was granted.

On the other hand, Jesus refused the request of the mother of James and John that her sons be placed, one at his right hand, the other at his left.

Parents are the first educators of their children. They have generally nursed their children through triumphs and heartache. Usually, the welfare of their children is uppermost in parents' minds.

Sometimes, when love turns to hatred, children can be used as ammunition in wars between parents; teachers and administrators can get caught in the crossfire.

We as teachers are called upon to recognise and respect the prior rights of parents, be they co-operative or 'difficult'. However, in fairness – or even legally – we cannot always agree to every request or concur in every judgment.

We obviously need wisdom and charity to deal with parents in a way that respects their rights, those of their children, and those of other parents and children.

Reflections

Teaching

Maurice Baring (1874-1945) is frequently described as a man of letters. While he was a prolific, if undistinguished, writer, he was certainly a distinguished companion and gentleman. A severe critic of one of his books observed that the central character was like Baring himself: 'a charming, clean, modest Englishman'.

In one of his novels, he describes a character in this way:

> Everything about him... gave the impression of centuries and hidden stores of pent-up civilisation.

This enviable depth of culture is probably beyond the reach of most of us, but the aspiration to be genuinely learned is a worthy one for teachers – for our own enrichment and to fire the ambitions of students.

We can all probably remember at least one teacher whose love of learning inspired us, and we acknowledge the good that she or he did us.

We might thank God for the teachers who inspired us, and ask for the ability to inspire our students to love learning and pursue truth, a quest that will always lead to God.

Teaching

> Speak first, as becomes your seniority, but with due choice of words; and do not break in when music is a-playing; no need for your words to flow when none is listening, for your wisdom to be displayed unnecessarily.
>
> Sirach 32:4-6

Efficient teaching is inseparable from the management of a class.

While the above advice comes from a set of counsels about conducting a feast, there are some points that are relevant to classroom management.

First, the teacher is in charge: this responsibility can never be shrugged off.

Second, like the host, the teacher needs to detect the rhythms of the class and not intervene when it is inopportune or when things are going quite well by themselves.

Third, a teacher needs to ensure that what is said is worthwhile.

There are, of course, many management techniques; the ones we adopt will depend on our personality, our style, and the class we have.

We seek the wisdom to adopt management strategies that suit us and secure a peaceful atmosphere for learning.

Teaching

> Accustom your son to the rod, because you love him; so you will have comfort of him in your later years.
> Sirach 30:1

A more familiar version of the above is 'Spare the rod and spoil the child'.

While the purpose of classroom management is that punishments take place rarely, to a greater or lesser extent they are part of the life of every school.

Most teachers try to be constructive: to help the student to be better. Some teachers punish to make themselves feel better.

Perhaps we can recall a time when we were punished unjustly or excessively: the memory can rankle for a lifetime.

We realise that hasty punishments, unkind words and humiliations are destructive.

We try to be discerning and moderate in the use of punishment.

Teaching

> We all heartily detested Sister Anastasie...
> From a memoir relating to schooling in nineteenth-century France.

(The memorialist here was a classmate of Bernadette Soubirous – St Bernadette of Lourdes.)

Whatever the content of Sister's lessons, students recalled only that they did not like her.

Perhaps she was ill, sick of teaching, unhappy, trapped...

The students may well have summed up all her deficiencies by saying that she was 'mean'.

This term includes vindictiveness, cruelty, relentlessness, victimisation: habitual conduct rather than isolated incidents.

We might pray for colleagues who feel themselves trapped in this way, for students who feel aggrieved, and ask for the strength to avoid being mean.

Teaching

> God has had the goodness... to establish... the Christian schools, where children are kept all day and learn reading, writing and their religion. In these schools, the children are always kept busy, so that when their parents want them to go to work, they are prepared for their employment.
> St John Baptist de La Salle (1651-1719), Patron of teachers.

Like all the founders of teaching orders, de La Salle was concerned that children should learn religious truths. He, and they, were also concerned that the children acquired the knowledge to make their way in society. All founders insisted that religion and the other subjects be taught well.

Curricula have changed but the Founders' vision has been kept alive by Sisters, Brothers and Priests, often in the face of great difficulties.

To adapt Isaac Newton's saying, we who are in schools now are standing on the shoulders of giants.

As we acknowledge the contribution which teaching Religious have made, we seek to share and implement their insights into fitting our students for life in today's society.

Teaching

> Now the Athenians in general and the foreigners there had no time for anything but talking or hearing about the latest novelty.
>
> Acts 17:21

It is essential for a teacher to keep abreast of advances in knowledge and pedagogy.

However, we must admit that over our teaching career we have seen many innovations come and go. Cupboards and bookshelves contain the flotsam and jetsam of many an educational tide.

Some three hundred years ago, a manual written for school children advised readers to be neither the first nor the last to adopt a new fashion. It sounds like good advice

This middle-of-the-road approach would lead us to avoid over-hasty acceptance on the one hand, and professional atrophy on the other.

We need a generous spirit and an open mind when opportunities for professional development come along.

Teaching

> Everyone has the right to this treasure.

Czeslaw Milosz (1911-2004) poet, academic, diplomat, Nobel laureate, asserted that all people have a right to the insights and the literary qualities of the Bible. It was with the same view that – a few years ago – a woman who is an atheist wrote an article in the *Spectator*, lamenting the fact that her son was not being taught the Bible.

The Catholic philosopher Jacques Maritain went further, considering that all the other great literary masterpieces, and the Bible, constitute the common good: the inheritance to which every human being has a right. Of course, we may include scientific and artistic achievements as well.

We hear much these days about social capital and cultural capital; and the need to facilitate an equitable sharing of them.

It is our privilege and our duty as teachers to help our students, according to their capacity, to share this common good.

We might give thanks to God who has given such great gifts to human beings and ask for the generosity to share our insights and knowledge, even when our audience is not particularly receptive.

Teaching

> ... it is necessary... that passivity be encouraged and assertiveness... be restricted... that lethargy be rewarded; that individuality be obliterated...
> From a report on prisons, quoted by Maisie Ward in her *To and Fro on the Earth*.

The report aimed to prove that certain prisons work on the principle that the prisoners can best be controlled by anaesthetising their spirit.

Some teachers may subscribe to this view.

Conversely, this kind of management may be favoured by a sizable group of students, who go along with schooling as long as it does not disrupt their comfort.

They are content forever to engage in low order activities.

They are agreeable, provided they are not pushed too hard. A recurring comment on their reports is 'could do better'.

This group in fact can erode the standards of the whole school, making mediocrity the norm and punishing any student whom they find to be 'unco guid'.

This cultivated inertia can be overcome only if all staff make a consistent and concerted effort to counter it.

Teaching

> ... let patience accomplish a perfect work.
> James 1:4

There are probably very few of us who can boast that we have never been impatient in class.

Some students irritate us by their thoughtlessness or immaturity. Some delight in stirring their teacher and such students are often adept at recruiting allies; their joint efforts can try the teacher's patience to breaking point.

Most of us are likely to admit that illness, lack of sleep, worries and so on can make us impatient. We may also admit that difficulties have arisen because our planning was not thorough enough.

We regret our failures in patience, and remember those who have suffered because of them.

Teaching

> There is a boy here who has five barley loaves and two fishes; but what is that among so many?
>
> John 6:9

At Mass, the little boy had been trying hard to be good. After Communion, he said 'Grandma, what was that round thing you had in your hand?' Evidently, he had little experience of Mass.

Perhaps at some time in the future, he will attend a Catholic school. Chances are that he will be unchurched, with little knowledge of, or even interest in, religious matters.

In his class, there will, of course, be many students who are thoroughly grounded in religious belief.

There may be others like the senior students who asked how they could 'get unbaptised'.

We know that God wants all of these students to be saved and come to the knowledge of the truth. One of the means that he will use is our religion lessons.

It is a great privilege to teach religion, but most of us frequently find it very hard going. We feel like St Andrew who spoke up and said that his resources were inadequate for the task confronting him.

At such times, it is helpful to remember that the God whom we serve, is, after all, all powerful.

We trust in God's power and love to preserve us from discouragement.

Teaching

> Doing the truth in charity...

Many of us teach religion. Others do not, either because the timetable does not allow it, or because we do not quite feel up to it.

Nevertheless, we all still share in the mission of the school. We are all engaged in seeking the truth, and in the quest to put the truth into practice in our lives.

We all know, as St Paul reminds us, that without charity, doing the truth would be pointless.

We know, too, that many of our colleagues who do not teach religion are fine role models in seeking truth and in the way they treat others.

We thank God for the diversity of gifts that we find around us and ask for the insight to appreciate the contributions which all our colleagues make to the life of the school.

Teaching

> Behave wisely towards those outside your own number; use the present opportunity to the full. Let your conversation be always gracious, and never insipid; study how best to talk with each person you meet.
>
> Colossians 4:5-6

Colossae was a small city of minor importance in what is now south-west Turkiye.

Its citizens were noted for their interest in various religions and their tendency to blend them.

Members of the small Christian community were converts from Judaism and the various pagan cults. Daily, these Christians rubbed shoulders with their non-Christian compatriots.

Paul did not urge his followers to shun them but rather to treat them graciously – and certainly not condescendingly.

We will certainly encounter students and colleagues whose views are poles apart from our own; sometimes they may be aggressive and bitter.

In such encounters, we do well to be mindful of Paul's advice.

Teaching

> It is certain that when he makes water his urine is congealed ice.
>
> Shakespeare, *Measure for Measure*

Angelo is thought to have so cooled his passions that even his urine is ice cold.

Such is not the case: behind a mask of virtue, he is plotting to seduce the virtuous Isabella.

Unfortunately, in our schools, there have been many examples of teachers using the screen of religion or professional activities to abuse children, many of whom suffer for life, even to the extent of killing themselves.

Such failures have often been covered up.

These are matters for shame and regret and reminders of our professional obligations.

Teaching

> The reed that is bruised he will not crush
> Or quench the smoldering wick...
>
> Matthew 12:20

After ordination, a certain priest's first appointment was to be a teacher.

He was exemplary in his priestly life, thoroughly competent in the subjects he was appointed to teach, and well prepared for his lessons.

He was a complete failure because of his inflexibility.

Fortunately, he moved to another apostolate, where he was so successful that he has been canonised.

We need the compassion to make allowances for the bruised reed and the smoldering wick – among our colleagues as well as among our students.

Teaching

> In durance vile here must I wake and weep
> Robert Burns (1759-1796)
>
> There is no jollitie but hath a smack of folly.
> George Herbert (1593-1633)

(Robert Burns was a Scottish poet. George Herbert was a poet and priest of the Church of England.)

When we teach next to some classrooms, we are aware that no sound ever escapes its walls. Students file in and out as if to and from a prison cell – durance vile.

On the other hand, we may well have witnessed a class where the students enter in high spirits and the lesson mounts to increasingly loud outbursts of jollity – perhaps bordering on folly.

We respect our colleagues' management techniques but it does not seem unreasonable to wonder about the impact these measures have on students.

Teaching

> You can't be serious...

In his novel, *Missionaries*, Phil Klay relates the fortunes of a group of people who, each on a personal mission. gather at a village on the Colombian border.

One of them is a general's daughter who is a university student; she seeks his permission to do a practicum with the poor and abandoned.

He replies that she had been sent to a Catholic school, taught to go to Mass to say her prayers and so on, but surely she doesn't believe 'in that shit'.

It is not improbable that we and our students will encounter people who are surprised that we take religion seriously. It is hard not to succumb to ridicule.

Teaching

> My grandfather, my mother, my great-grandfather, my tutor, my teachers, my housekeeper, my adoptive father, my brother, the gods...

As he looked back over his life, these are some of the people the emperor Marcus Aurelius (121-180 AD) thanked for their beneficial influence on his life and outlook.

In addition to his role as emperor, he developed his understanding as a Stoic philosopher.

His reflections, now known as *Meditations*, have been, and are, respected as guides to rational conduct.

The above list is extracted from Book 1 of his reflections.

It is a reminder that many people influence our students .

We acknowledge with gratitude the members of other professions who work beside us: chaplains, nurses, counsellors, accountants...

Teaching

> Since he had to pass through Samaria, he came to a town called Sychar...
>
> John 4:4

Ill feeling between Jews and Samaritans had a long history. When groups of Jews returned after captivity in Babylon in the sixth century BC, they found in Samaria remnants who had developed different teachings and had married people from other races. Their temple on Mt Gerizim, where they worshipped rather than in the temple at Jerusalem, was later destroyed by the Jews.

Thus when Jesus came to the Samaritan town, Sychar, almost 50 km north of Jerusalem, he met a hostile reception.

When a Samaritan woman came to the well, in reply to Jesus' request for a drink she said, 'How can you, a Jew ask me a Samaritan woman for a drink?'

Sometimes, we may be allocated a Religion class which, for some reason, is hostile to religion and unwilling to co-operate.

Like Jesus before us, we have to begin with some basic, shared need that has no immediate connection with religion – like something to drink. Like him we may find our first step rejected.

We need patience and resourcefulness

Teaching

> 'Go, call your husband and come back here.'
> 'I have no husband.'
>
> John 4:16

Jesus had tried, unsuccessfully, to alert the Samaritan woman to the wider significance of 'living water' but she was really not interested.

Back to basics: she certainly was interested in the topic of her husband(s), and so, when she saw that Jesus understood the reality of her life a dialogue was initiated, to the extent that she recalled some of her religious beliefs, and acknowledged his perceptiveness: 'I see that you are a prophet'.

When she described her encounter to others in Sychar, she did not report about worshipping God in spirit but that Jesus had told her everything about herself. Her compatriots were thus inspired to go and see Jesus for themselves.

It is a great gift to be able to find common ground.

Teaching

> At this point the disciples returned and were surprised to find him conversing with a woman.
> His disciples were pleading with him 'Rabbi, eat, please'.
> 'I have food to eat of which you are ignorant.'
> [They] said among themselves 'Did someone bring him something to eat?'
>
> John 4:27, 31-33

The apostles, who had gone into the town to buy food, returned to find him talking to the Samaritan woman. It all seemed too hard for them so they concentrated on trying to get him to eat.

Jesus took the occasion to point out to them that they had a wider mission than finding food. The fields 'are white and ripe for the harvest...I am sending you to reap...'

(He was still trying to enlighten them at the Last Supper, when he prayed, 'I also pray for those who through their teaching will believe in me'.)

Jesus adds, ' One does the planting, another the reaping'.

Maybe we sow, or maybe we reap, or maybe we do neither. We may feel that we are like Jesus in another setting when those whom he was teaching 'picked up stones to throw at him'.

We pray to the Lord of the harvest for all who work for him – ourselves included.

Teaching

> As there were false prophets among the people of Israel, so among you there will be false teachers, who secretly introduce destructive errors
>
> 2 Peter 2:1

Of course, the writer is not alluding to the classroom, but to the Christian community. Right from the outset, there have been those who come up with their own interpretations and spread them among believers.

Such is still the case: we need to 'guard lest you be carried away by [the] lawless...'

Some people laud the lawless as radical reformers while others condemn them and side with conservative spokespersons.

We strive to be loyal to the truth rather than to personalities.

Teaching

> 'You ain't heard nothing yet.'

With these words in *The Jazz Singer* in 1927, Al Jolson ushered in the use of sound and dialogue in motion pictures.

They were also used for a different purpose by a boy in a senior class in a Catholic school.

He took it as his mission to make a certain teacher's life unbearable. When one of his classmates urged him to ease up, he replied, 'You ain't heard nothing yet'.

And so it proved to be. (Maybe this disposition enabled him later to climb the political ladder and become a government minister.)

After we make every allowance, we have to be honest and acknowledge that some students can be nasty. In days gone by, they were either forced to comply or be excluded.

Most observers will agree that there has been an increase in serious misbehaviour in class: refusing to obey directions, insults, swearing and violence.

The teacher confronted by the senior boy years ago was very experienced; he had a reputation for outwitting difficult students. In this case, he was defeated.

Many teachers feel defeated these days.

Obviously, systemic remedies are needed. In the meantime, schools need to close ranks, coming up with shared strategies to protect colleagues and the majority of students, who still want to learn.

Teaching

> I dare thee, coward, to maintain this wrong
> At dint of rapier, single in the field.
> Robert Greene, *Friar Bacon and Friar Bungay*, 1594

This challenge to a duel was accepted, with disastrous consequences. Like many challenges, it was ill-conceived, a delusion. We have no doubt seen cases where people have pursued foolish dreams.

We have also seen many people ennobled by facing up to challenges in relationships, physical or mental sufferings and handicaps and so on.

We know that even in the most orderly of schools, teaching has its challenges.

We make the effort to broaden and deepen our professional competence.

If we teach RE, we try to deepen our knowledge of, and our commitment to, following Christ Our Lord.

We co-operate with our colleagues in facing emerging challenges in society.

Teaching

> Remain here and keep on watching...
> And he came and found them sleeping...
> 'Get up! Let us go. Look, the one who has betrayed me has come near...'
> And they all left him and fled.
>
> Mark 14:38-50

We are not Wonder Woman or Superman.

The spirit is willing but the flesh is weak: despite our best intentions, at times we can fail to measure up to challenges facing us.

We ask the Lord for forgiveness and the grace – like the apostles – to return and fight on.

Teaching

> A square peg in a round hole.

Over the years, we will have encountered colleagues who were totally unsuited to teaching.

Some may have been eccentrics and we recall their words and exploits with gentle amusement.

Others – in their unhappiness and lack of engagement with students and the school – may have caused suffering to themselves and others.

We wish them happiness in a calling more suited to them

God bless them all!

Teaching

> Remember, O Lord, your servants N. and N., who have gone before us with the sign of faith, and rest in the sleep of peace. Grant them, O Lord we pray, and all who sleep in Christ, a place of refreshment, light and peace.
>
> Eucharistic Prayer I

We are aware of the death of students, colleagues and parents.

Some will have been close to us; with others, sad to say, we may have had disagreements that were not resolved.

We forgive and ask for forgiveness.

We pray for them all, and in particular for those whom we remember by name on this occasion.

8

On care: the work of mind and heart

> Two things are required of [a Good Shepherd as regards his sheep]: to be responsible for them and to love them; one is not enough without the other.
>
> St Thomas Aquinas

('Care' here includes 'pastoral care', 'vigilance', 'guidance', 'correction', 'watchfulness', affection...' In some instances, it can include 'crisis management'.)

Drawing upon rich and frequent allusions in the scriptures, Jesus spoke of himself as the Good Shepherd. As we all know, the Latin word for shepherd is 'pastor' and those who share in Jesus' work (particularly bishops and priests) are said to acts as pastors and to exhibit pastoral characteristics.

Many writers attribute to Pope St Gregory the Great the coining of the term 'pastoral care' because of the treatise The Book of Pastoral Rule, which he wrote in 590, shortly after his election. The work was written in response to a Bishop's request for guidance in handling his flock.

In education, the term became common in the mid-1950s, though teachers have always practised pastoral care, even if the terminology was not familiar. These days, some members of the staff of a school exercise pastoral care in a variety of professional ways, for example as administrators, chaplains, counselors and nurses. But, of course, pastoral care is a duty for all teachers and other members of staff.

Moreover, the legal responsibilities of a teacher and indeed those of most other people who deal with the public, are often derived from a 'duty of care'.

The focus here is on the classroom, where 'care' is a term which is a synthesis of the ideas expressed by the sayings 'to keep an eye on', 'to look out for', 'to have a special regard for', 'to watch over' and 'guard me as the apple of your eye'.

Care

> I don't want to play in your yard,
> I don't like you anymore...
>
> Dick Manning, Henry. W. Petrie, Philip Wingate (1894)

These, the first lines of the chorus in a song which tells the tale of a falling out between two young girls, have over the years been used to convey adult angst following a break up.

But, as we know only too well, a break up between children, young or old, can cause a great deal of suffering. The break up may be temporary and quickly patched up, or it can deteriorate into a vendetta, involving others and social media. Some children may, therefore, refuse to come to school, or become depressed, or retaliate violently, or...

Sometimes after an outbreak of violence or intimidation at school or through social media, parents will say, 'Why doesn't the school do something about it?' A school may indeed fail in a duty of care. But we know that despite our best efforts and the implementation of action plans, threats, counselling and cajoling, students can devise ways of slipping through our defences.

One of the many challenges facing today's teachers.

Care

> Give therefore to thy servant an understanding heart, to judge thy people and to discern between good and evil.
>
> 1 Kings 3:9

Watchful care involves the mind and heart: a coldly intellectual approach would be as deficient as one that is overly emotional.

Solomon's prayer for an understanding heart is thus a helpful reminder of the synthesis required.

Obviously, we cannot *feel* affection for every child, but we can aim at displaying warmth to all. Moreover, the exercise of care needs to be well thought out – it needs to be wise.

We might adopt Solomon's prayer for a heart that understands.

Care

> He then went down in their company and came to Nazareth, where he was subject to them... Jesus made steady progress, proportionately to his age, in understanding and in favour with God and people.
>
> Luke 2:51, 52.

The various professions undertake pastoral care in a way suited to their modality. Thus, a doctor's care differs from that of a chaplain. The pastoral care practised by teachers is different again.

We have no way of knowing exactly what Jesus did in Nazareth, except that he lived in a family and took part in the life of his village. Under this type of care and tutelage, he developed his understanding and his other powers in a way that pleased God and fellow villagers.

This kind of development is of the same kind that can take place in a school. The watchfulness and the progressive instruction which Jesus experienced is of the same type that teachers and a school can offer.

We might ask Our Lady to help us deal with our students so that their understanding develops and that they acquire those qualities that please God and others.

Care

> ... dark be the valley about my path, hurt I feel none while he is with me; thy rod, thy crook are my comfort.
>
> Psalm 22:4

The 'rod' was in fact a club, often iron tipped, to ward off wolves, jackals and the like; the crook was used to guide the sheep and retrieve them if they fell.

Thus, the shepherd protected the sheep from physical danger and rescued them if necessary.

The supportive teacher performs the same functions.

If we are looking after small children, it is obvious that the teacher sometimes stands between them and physical danger, and the steps to be taken are usually quite clear.

With older children, it is not so much the threat of physical danger at school, but the results of 'outside' activities that are of concern. We learn about them from the students themselves, on the grapevine, or from parents. We wonder just how far our responsibility extends, particularly if the danger cannot be proven with certainty. We worry whether saying something or acting in a certain way is going to make things worse; we realise that to make an accusation where no fault has occurred can do much harm.

Discretion and tact are called for.

Care

> [Teachers] should understand that their first duty is to watch over students... to prevent them falling into evil rather than to punish them when they have fallen.
>
> *Ratio Studiorum.*

The *Ratio Studiorum* is a Jesuit manual of educational procedures, first published in 1599. The above quotation is taken from a nineteenth-century German edition.

Often, a quiet word will help a child to see the direction in which he or she is heading, and help them to alter course.

Perhaps, we ourselves can look back with gratitude to the teacher who took the trouble to speak to us kindly in this way. Or, perhaps, we recall the rebuke that pulled us back into line. We may have been surprised that the teacher knew us so well.

We are grateful to the teachers who guided us, and seek the tact and discernment to make the right comment at the right time.

Care

> I myself will tend my flock, I myself will pen them in their fold, says the Lord God. I will search for the lost, recover the straggler, bandage the hurt, strengthen the sick, leave the healthy and strong to play, and give them their proper food.
>
> Ezekiel 34:15-16

Groups of Jews were deported to Babylon from about 600BC to 538BC.

Among their number was the prophet Ezekiel and his wife. They died there.

While many of Ezekiel's prophecies were critical of the behaviour of his countrymen, he also tried to encourage them. The most well-known prophecy is the vision of the dry bones (Ezekeil 37:1-14) which taught that God would bring new life to the exiles.

The passage quoted above is a striking statement that pastoral care involves the weak and the strong – all our students in fact.

Care

> Whence every teacher also, that they may edify all in the one virtue of charity, ought to touch the hearts of their hearers out of one doctrine, but not with the one and the same exhortation.
>
> Pope St Gregory, *The Pastoral Rule*

Pope Gregory then goes on to enumerate many instances where people must be spoken to appropriately: men differently from women; the poor differently from the rich; the joyful from the sad; the learned from the ignorant, and many more.

Catering for personal differences lies at the heart of pastoral care. To quote Jesuit sources again, the relevant term is 'cura personalis', personal care.

Insights and patience are needed to make allowances for the individuality of our students.

Care

> I am the good shepherd; my sheep are known to me and know me; just as I am known to my Father, and know him.
>
> John 10:14-15

Children adduce many reasons for liking teachers: they are attuned to the rhythms of the class (though not in those words!); the teacher engages and enlarges interest: the teacher keeps the class in order without duress; good humour prevails in the teacher's class...

On a one-to-one basis, children will identify their special teacher by saying 'He/she understands me'.

Here, too, Jesus is our model.

We might thank the Lord for understanding us as an individual, with a name known only to the two of us, and ask that we be granted the insights and generosity to work towards knowing our students individually.

Care

> They have no wine left.
>
> John 2:4

Jesus and his disciples attended a wedding at Cana which was only a few kilometres from Nazareth. The bridal party would have been relatives or friends of Mary and Jesus.

What an embarrassment it would have been for the young couple and their families to run out of wine at a wedding reception!

No doubt Our Lady knew the circumstances of the host family; it is probable that she was keeping an eye on things and thus intervened in time to prevent them from losing face.

Jesus seemed to be reluctant to intervene, but he did so generously in quality and quantity.

It was all done so quietly that the MC had no idea what had happened.

Our Lady is here the very model of watchful care.

Care

> Yet Edmund was belov'd...
> ... Some good I mean to do
> Despite of mine own nature.
>
> King Lear, Act V, Sc iii.

Edmund made no bones about being evil; he ridiculed those who blamed their malice on external forces like the stars.

He was loved by two sisters who had dispositions similar to his own. They killed each other out of love for him.

Twisted as this love was, it was love, and as Edmund lay dying, it inspired him to do something good, even though it went against the grain.

We are obliged to distinguish truth from falsehood and good from evil, but not to judge others' moral worth: we are to leave that to God.

In our contact with our students, we will at times be struck by the generosity of the most unlikely children. We can only bow in wonder at the workings of God's plans.

Care

> And he said to them, 'Come away into a quiet place by yourselves and rest a little'. For there were many coming and going, and they scarcely had leisure even to eat.
>
> Mark 6:31

While the first objects of our care are the children confided to us, charity demands that we do not lose sight of the needs of the adults with whom we associate.

In times of grief, stress or illness, our colleagues need our help.

There are many occasions when we will come across parents who are hurting badly.

According to our position in the school, our ability, and our access to resources, we can imitate the Lord by taking practical steps that show we care.

Care

> I am just going outside and I may be some time.
>
> Lawrence Oates.

In 1912, Oates and three others were returning from the South Pole. They were badly affected by the cold and their supplies were well-nigh exhausted.

On his thirty-second birthday, when the outside temperature was -40 degrees, he crawled out of their tent, in a gesture that has been interpreted as the sacrifice of his life for others.

He was capable both of heroic deeds and of those that were shameful. We will never know whether he was practising the ultimate act of care, or whether his physical injuries drove him to suicide. Possibly his motive was a mixture of both.

Jesus believed that there was no greater test of love than to lay down one's life for one's friends.

We may pray that we recognise the true motives of our caring and that we develop the selflessness of which Jesus spoke.

Care

> Little deeds of kindness, little words of love,
> Help to make earth happy, like the heaven above.
>
> From *Little Things*, by Julia A. Carney (1823-1908)

Julia Carney was an American primary school teacher. In 1845, at a teachers' conference, she and the rest of the group were given a ten-minute writing exercise. By chance, she had written the first few lines of a poem the night before and used the ten minutes to finish it. It was later included in a popular school reader, and thus became known to many pupils and teachers.

The language may not be fashionable these days, but the assertion of the importance of kindness remains valid.

We can probably look back on an occasion when someone, out of the blue, did us the very act of kindness of which we stood most in need. We wondered how the person was able to read our need so well.

We may even have said that it was a godsend, which, of course, it ultimately was.

Such occasions are moments when we become especially aware of grace.

Remembering the kindnesses we have received, we might give thanks for them, pray for those who helped us so, and ask that we be ever ready to perform little acts of kindness for the students confided to our care.

Reflections

Care

> ... Mary had been espoused to Joseph; but before they lived together, it was found that she was pregnant by the Holy Spirit. Joseph, her husband, being right-minded, and unwilling to expose her, resolved to put her away without public formalities.
>
> Matthew 1:18-20

Older translations rendered 'right-minded' as 'just'. According to strict justice, the law would have been on Joseph's side had he chosen to make a great display of renouncing Mary.

Instead of justice, he chose mercy.

Older school management manuals used to advise that sometimes it is better for a teacher to pretend that some infraction has not been seen: inexorable punishment is in no one's best interest. Many of us gratefully recall someone who cared enough about us to overlook what we had done.

At times, students – or a staff member – are thought to have failed so seriously that people howl for them to be punished. Punishment may indeed be called for; if we really care about the person, we should consider whether mercy is also warranted.

Care

> Learn, rather, how to do good, setting your hearts on justice, righting the wrong, protecting the orphan, giving the widow redress...
>
> Isaiah 1:17

When Isaiah was prophesying around 700 BC, an invasion was looming.

Orphans and widows had few resources, few if any supporters, and were thus among the most vulnerable members of society.

Experience shows that, these days, schools usually rally around widows and orphans.

In every school, however, there are students who are 'orphans' – with few resources, friends or negotiable skills, they are very vulnerable.

Students may be in this position because of their appearance, their mannerisms, their disabilities, their nationality, or their home life. They are often ridiculed and bullied.

Other students are isolated because they are easily irritated and others delight in tormenting them until the flash point is reached.

There are also some students who, adept at annoying teachers and other students, are impervious to advice and other steps taken to help them.

It is very difficult to help all these kinds of students: we try to get 'good' students to include them in their groups; we try to deal with the bullies to release the victims from pressure; we may take them under our wing, but what these students really crave is the companionship of their peers. Sadly, some students' school days pass without any peer support at all. Their days pass in misery.

Frequently, we have to act case by case and from day to day.

We might pray for the ability to create a supportive, inclusive, classroom atmosphere, and ask for compassion and patience.

Care

> Turn a deaf ear... to the blandishments of evil doers that would make you join their company.
> Proverbs 1:10

Every teacher can remember cases where students have gone downhill because they fell in with the wrong crowd.

The attraction of their peers' support and esteem is so strong for children that it is hard to wean them away.

It is also hard – and risky – to say to a child, 'I think you should stay away from so and so'. The student will ask 'Why?' Great tact is necessary to frame a reply.

This is a circumstance where we have an important watching brief so that we can take early action to save the situation.

Care

> Liberation of the oppressed… liberation of the oppressors.

It is our hope that, inspired by the teachings they receive at school and by the behaviour they observe there, our students will commit themselves to relieve the sufferings of the oppressed.

The Lutheran theologian, Jurgen Moltmann, reflected upon the liberation of oppressors: if only they could be liberated from their obsessions, then they well might stop their works of oppression.

We are aware that, through technology, the opportunities for students' oppression of one another goes far beyond name calling in the yard or a punch up behind the lockers.

The problem is complex, not admitting of simple – and certainly not of simplistic – solutions.

We might find it helpful to try to find out what makes the oppressors tick, and work on that.

In any case, we might pray for our oppressed and oppressive students.

Care

> The screw may twist and the rack may turn...
> W. S. Gilbert, *Yeomen of the Guard*

In every profession, there are duties that can be excruciatingly tedious – 'boring' is a word often invoked in such circumstances.

Invigilation of a long exam leads us to study spots on the ceiling.

Supervision in the playground can be tedious, particularly when the weather is oppressive, or when our replacement is late or does not turn up. Nevertheless, our presence can help to prevent mischief, sometimes harmless, other times, malicious.

Some teachers readily socialise with students, while other teachers, by nature aloof, are rather solitary figures.

It is not unknown for some teachers to be regularly late, or to skip supervision entirely, or to spend the time checking their mobile phone.

We cannot shirk this duty.

We brace ourselves to perform this and other tedious duties in a proper professional manner.

9

On witness: delivering the message by word and deed

> At that particular time, he had cured many people of diseases, afflictions, and evil spirits, and made many people happy by granting them sight. So, taking advantage of the opportunity, he said to them: 'Go and bring word to John about all you see and hear: the blind recover sight, the lame walk, lepers are made clean, the deaf hear, the dead rise again, the humble have the Good News preached to them'.
>
> Luke 7:21-22

Jesus pointed out to John's followers that he was doing precisely what he was required to do: his actions spoke for themselves; his words were matched by his deeds.

His actions were also lessons: 'I have been setting you an example, which will teach you in turn to do what I have done for you' (John 13:15).

There are many sayings which make the point: 'Actions speak louder than words', 'Practise what you preach', 'Example is better than precept', etc.

Conversely, there are few words more insulting than to be called hypocrites or frauds.

Obviously, it is ridiculous to teach students to behave in a certain way if we they see us consistently doing or standing for the opposite.

We are challenged to live according to the Gospel but sometimes we may be only too aware that our actions have not reflected the values we profess.

The truth of the matter is that we will often fail – 'All of us often go wrong' – as St James reminds us. We will be impatient, impulsive, and so on. Students can distinguish between isolated acts and habit, between words said in the heat of the moment, and those motivated by malice, between honest expressions of belief and waffle. In short, despite our shortcomings they can tell what we really stand for.

We are all members of the pilgrim Church, not of the company of saints in heaven.

We can try to bear witness to Christian behaviour, fail and try again. It is recorded that the great St Francis used to say, 'Let us begin again'.

Witness

> As far as an atheist can pray, I am praying for you.
>
> A message sent to Pope John XXIII in his last illness.

Although he had his critics, many people called this pope 'Good Pope John'.

He had the ability to communicate good will and goodness. He made people hope. He matched his words with his deeds. People who met him were inclined to say, 'There might be something in it, after all'. His humanity led them to listen.

We might pray to Saint John XXIII for the ability to touch hearts as he did.

Witness

> I have lived for Christ. I want to die for Christ.
> Last words of Sr Restituta Kafka (1894-1943).

Sister Restituta was guillotined during the Nazi regime in Vienna.

Other Sisters gave her the nickname of 'Resoluta', because she was so strong-willed.

She was a very competent nurse and anaesthetist.

Restituta fell foul of the authorities because she insisted on displaying the Crucifix and praying with the dying. (She also refused to take Hitler seriously.)

In prison, she continued to care for the sick; she shared her rations with those she judged more needy than herself.

It was Martin Bormann himself who, seeing the impact of her example, ordered her execution.

Like Blessed Restituta, we try to do what we profess.

Witness

> How can we expect righteousness to prevail when there is hardly anyone willing to give themself up individually to a righteous cause?
> Sophie Scholl (1921-1943)

Sophie Scholl was executed in the same way as Sr Restituta, in 1943.

This young Lutheran woman was a member of an underground group called The White Rose. Striving to stir the conscience of the German people, they published newsletters critical of the regime.

She, her brother, and another member were captured and executed as traitors. She was 21.

In his career as executioner, Johann Reichart guillotined three thousand prisoners; he declared that Sophie Scholl was the bravest of them all.

The Scholls are looked upon as heroes of conscience.

Witness

> This is how we spoke to them, not with words but with our hands and our actions... there we sat, or rather knelt, beside them and bathed their faces and bodies with wine. We made every effort to encourage them with friendly gestures and displayed in their presence the emotions which somehow tend to hearten the sick.
> St Peter Claver (1581-1654)

Peter Claver was a Spaniard who worked in Cartagena in what is now Colombia. It was a hub of the slave trade.

The quotation above is taken from a letter he wrote in 1627. By that time, he had been working with slaves for thirteen years and he was to continue this work for another twenty-seven years.

The slaves, described as coming from Guinea, arrived after a voyage of horrors in which up to a third of the 'cargo' perished at sea. When they arrived, they were herded into pens to be examined by prospective buyers. The sick and dying were left on the ground, and these were the people who were Claver's first concern.

He lifted them out of the mud, placed them near a fire, covered them and then ministered to them in the way described above.

When people's immediate needs are met, they are likely to believe that someone is interested in them. They may then show some interest in what inspired their benefactors; even if they don't, much good has been accomplished.

Witness

> Is your duty preaching and teaching? Consider carefully what is required to fulfil that office fittingly. Make sure in the first place that your life and conduct are sermons in themselves. Do not give people cause to purse their lips and shake their heads during your sermons, since they have heard you before preaching one thing —and then seen you do the exact opposite.
>
> St Charles Borromeo

Borromeo (1538-1584) was the Cardinal Archbishop of Milan. Among his many good works, he established schools for the poor and instituted Sunday schools.

His words are so obviously true that they need no elaboration, except to say that we may recall pursing our lips (or the equivalent) when someone's lessons to us were not reflected in the person's conduct.

Witness

> First he did and afterwards he taught:
> From the Gospel that truth he caught.
>
> Geoffrey Chaucer, *The Canterbury Tales*.

Chaucer's Canterbury Tales, written around 1400, describes a group of English pilgrims, and recounts the stories told to fill in time as they travelled along. The quotations given here are from the Prologue, where each of the pilgrims was described.

In the above quotation, Chaucer was describing a poor Parson (parish priest).

Chaucer went on to say:

It is a shame – let priests these words keep –
To see a filthy shepherd tending spotless sheep.

Virtuous as the Parson was

He was to sinful men not full of scorn
His speech was not a blasting horn
Rather, was it courteous and benign
For to draw folk to heaven, this was his design:
With good example kindness to combine.

Witness

> ... every preacher should give forth a sound more by his deed than by his words, and rather by good living imprint footsteps for people to follow than by speaking show them the way to walk in.
>
> Pope St Gregory, *The Book of Pastoral Rule*.

The founder of one of the religious teaching orders was wealthy in his own right. Once, when he was telling his early followers to bear poverty patiently, they replied that it was all right for him to talk: he had money to fall back on, whereas they had nothing.

He realised that they were right and proceeded to give his wealth away.

No doubt there have been many times when we have realised that students, colleagues or parents outdo us in their goodness, indeed, even in their good sense.

Sometimes, rather than being taught by us, our students teach us, and the reversal is not always easy to take.

Witness

> As he went from one bench to another, offering corrections, you had the feeling that here was a soul united to God and always perfectly composed.

This is an extract from a student's recollections of art lessons conducted by St Mutien-Marie Wiaux, a Belgian, who died in 1917.

His introduction to teaching was so shaky that some members of staff thought that he should be sent away. A senior member of staff offered to take him under his wing, and in time Mutien became quite competent in his work.

Working all his life in a large boarding school, in addition to his teaching, he did a great deal of supervision, a task for which there were few other takers.

He spent his life as a classroom teacher. The above testimony is but one of many that bore witness to the impact of his example.

Witness

> ... loaves of bread, a stolen limousine, the leg of a table, a bicycle, and a nun's habit.

These were some of the items that were used by the French saboteur Robert de la Rochefoucauld (1923-2012).

Accounts of his exploits and escapes as a member of the French Underground during World War II read like an adventure story. He was awarded high French and British honours. He was courage and resourcefulness personified.

It is said that the terms 'saboteur' and 'sabotage' come from some Belgian workers' practice of throwing a clog or 'sabot' into a machine to disrupt the work of a factory.

Sabotage can occur in schools, not by throwing wooden shoes, but by teachers' insidious behaviour or their propagation of ideas contrary to those articulated by the school.

Discernment is needed by administrators, and, hopefully, also by those who feel compelled to propagate ideas opposed to the school's stated objectives.

Witness

> All people are born as originals, but some die as photocopies.
>
> Carlo Acutis (1991-2006)

Carlo was fifteen when he died of leukemia.

In his short life, he was known as a computer whiz, defender of the bullied, consoler of friends whose parents were going through divorce, daily communicant and devotee of the Blessed Sacrament.

He also had the interests of a typical teenager.

In word and deed, he was a witness to the Christian ideal.

Hopefully, it has been our good fortune to have taught (and possibly influenced) such a student.

Witness

> She was unfailingly true to an age that was false to the core...
>
> Mark Twain, *Personal Recollections of Joan of Arc* (1896)

Joan of Arc (1412-1431) commanded an army at age seventeen, ensured that the French monarch was crowned, was tried for heresy, was found guilty and burned at the stake aged nineteen, posthumously exonerated and finally canonised.

She is one of the patrons of France; the Cross of Lorraine that was on the standard she carried has become a symbol embraced by the French in victory and defeat.

She has fascinated hundreds of writers, musicians, painters and sculptors.

One such writer was Mark Twain, usually remembered as the creator of Tom Sawyer and Huckleberry Finn. He had little esteem for the French, and even less for French Catholics but he was smitten with Joan and what she stood for. He considered that his testimony to her, the *Personal Recollections...* was his best work.

Witness

> Example isn't another way to teach; it's the only way to teach.
>
> Albert Einstein

The mother of several children tells the following story at her own expense.

One day, when she was working in the kitchen and her children were playing in the back yard with other children from the neighbourhood, she heard a voice pipe up: 'Let's play mummies and daddies'.

The voice belonged to her eldest child, who immediately continued: 'I'll be the mummy. Here you (pulling her by the arm), come and sweep the floor. You (pulling his ear), you just go and put out the rubbish. And you (a boy slinking away), don't think you're getting away with it, you're going to go up and do the messages. And you...'

It is pleasing when we suspect that our example may have been useful to others, upsetting when we realise that it is being belittled, and a source of sincere regret when we fear that it has led someone astray.

Witness

> To take the King's shilling.

In eighteenth-century England, men who volunteered to join the army were given the bonus of a shilling. In accepting it, they pledged loyalty to King and country.

People choosing employment in a Catholic school come with differing backgrounds, be they Catholics or members of another, or no, denomination.

It is reasonable for them all to respect the ethos of the school that employs them and act accordingly.

Witness

> Later on, therefore, when you have recovered, it is for you to strengthen your brothers and sisters.
>
> Luke 22:32

In betraying the Lord, Peter gave very bad example, and as St Paul was to point out, he did so again when he sided with the faction that would have imposed Jewish practices on pagan converts. Paul challenged him face-to-face.

Both men were profoundly convinced that God is rich in mercy, so that whatever our lapses, we will find forgiveness and the strength to try harder to support others.

Witness

> Berserk, amok, hysterical… tantrum, hissy fit, lost it

These words from different cultures demonstrate that an uncontrollable outburst is a long-standing, widespread form of human behaviour.

We may have endured it when our children were two-year-olds and we coped as best we could, or we feel sympathy at the supermarket, where a child's parents are frustrated and embarrassed by their infant's behaviour.

In the classroom or playground, tantrums are quite another matter.

Older children and adolescents who throw a tantrum most likely need expert intervention.

If we are not expert, but first on the scene, we obviously need to avoid our own emotional extremes by panicking. We need to try to isolate the child for his or her safety and that of others. It is quite futile to attempt reasoning with him or her.

It is not unknown that adults can act hysterically. We may be the first on the scene when a colleague or parent acts in this way.

Until an expert or support arrives, we try to be calm, patient, tolerant and prudent. A quick prayer will not go unanswered.

Later, the child or adult may act as if nothing had ever happened. Perhaps we best leave it this way.

10

On cultural awareness: reading the signs of the times

> A person's own sins are the instruments of their punishments... It would have been easy to send a plague of bears upon them, or noble lions; or to form new creatures of a ferocity hitherto unknown...but no, all you do is done in exact measure, all is nicely calculated and weighed.
>
> Wisdom 11:16-18, 21

In recalling the seven plagues inflicted in the time of Moses, the writer of the Book of Wisdom drew attention to the fact that rather than introducing exotic creatures the plagues involved things familiar to the culture of the Egyptians, making the punishments intelligible to them.

As Pope John Paul II pointed out, God communicates with us through our culture: the language, customs, symbols and values that set our society apart from others.

The writer of the Book of Wisdom would not have known of the word 'culture', but he or she would certainly have understood John Paul's idea: even God's displeasure is made known through things familiar to people.

Every culture contains much that is good and bad.

As teachers, we need to communicate through our culture, helping students to understand what is worthwhile in it, to discern its shortcomings, and to work to make it better.

In this way, we will be carrying out what the Congregation for Catholic Education calls 'the critical communication of culture'.

Cultural awareness

> The English, mad dogs. and all that...

According to the performer and playwright Noel Coward (1899-1973), Indians considered that only their English masters were silly enough to share the midday sun with dogs gone mad. but the aphorism seems to have been coined by Rudyard Kipling (1865-1936).

Kipling was born in India and worked there as a journalist for some years. His experiences fed his imagination and inspired many of his poems, stories and novels. There have been at least thirty movies based on his works. Many of us will remember The Jungle Book from our childhood and perhaps we were required to memorise his poem "If".

Although the final line from his poem "Recessional" (Lest we forget-lest we forget) is well known, his works have fallen out of favour because of perceptions of colonialism and racism in them.

Nevertheless, the quotation clearly expresses the gap that can be perceived when those in authority - teachers and schools for example - seem to be unaware of the way in which the realities of life are considered in the community in which they work.

Cultural awareness

> 'kid' 'togs' 'snitch' 'ridgy-didge' 'snooze'

Many of the convicts transported to Australia were professional thieves, who used their own argot or language (described as cant or 'flash') to conceal their plans and actions from outsiders.

Some of their terms. like the above, have passed into use by the wider community.

It is said that when some of the felons who made extensive use of flash language were hauled before a magistrate, an interpreter had to be called so that judge, accused and witnesses could understand each other.

Each culture has its own set of symbols or codes. Each culture has subcultures, each with its own codes. Outsiders have to learn the codes to communicate and win acceptance.

And so it is with schools.

Cultural awareness

> "The Fuzzy-Wuzzy Angels"

This is the title of a poem written in 1944 by Sapper Bert Beros when he was a soldier fighting on the Kokoda Track.

He was celebrating the loyalty and gallantry of the native Papuans (as they were then known) in carrying supplies and, more notably, the wounded, whom they ferried back to base, regardless of the dangers in which they found themselves.

"Fuzzy wuzzy" was a term of endearment in this poem, and in the language of the soldiers and the Australian people generally at that time.

We would not use the term these days because it sounds condescending and racist.

Some people find statues of certain nineteenth-century leaders and explorers offensive.

Thus, some cultural words and symbols are laden with conflicting significance.

Some are cancelled, that is, declared black. (That term might also be cancelled.)

Our students benefit from the example of our discernment and sensitivity.

Cultural awareness

> I have always had school sickness as others have sea sickness. I cried when it was time to go back to school.
>
> Jacques Derrida (1930-2004)

Born to a Jewish family in Algeria, Derrida, like other Jewish children, was excluded from state schools by the Vichy government. He refused to go to the school which the Jewish community established. Nevertheless, he eventually went on to achieve academic distinction.

He challenged the assumptions underlying Western culture and the process of 'deconstruction' associated with his name has been widely adopted.

Children of all ages are led to consider the validity of common assumptions.

Catholic schools are called upon to engage in the critical communication of culture, but not to abandon what is good, beautiful and true.

There is wisdom in the saying about throwing out the baby with the bath water.

Cultural awareness

> Pariah... outcast... untouchable.

'On the nose' is an expression that could be applied to any of the above terms.

People may be thought of being on the nose because of their religion, appearance, mannerisms and so on.

People can be born into a family or grouping of pariahs, deemed so because of their race or religion or illegal behaviour. They may live in an adopted or forced ghetto.

Some children with a parentage of alcoholism or drug addiction are born into a caste of disadvantage.

All of these people and many others may be considered as marginalised.

We realise that children from such backgrounds in our schools need to be treated with compassion and prudence.

Cultural awareness

> ... the black vomit in Paris who propagate decrees inspired by a corrupt moral code generated in dives to endorse rubbish.
>
> Léon Bloy, *La Femme Pauvre*, (1897)

In his novel about a poor and unfortunate woman, Clotilde, Bloy aired his opinions about painting, music, literature and society generally.

He evidently had little time for the trendies of his day.

Were he alive today, he would probably feel the same about trolls, some influencers, and others who use social media to propagate rubbish, not to mention spiteful outbursts.

Some students create such messages; many suffer from them. It is not unknown for teachers to be thus pilloried.

There is clearly a call for Catholic schools to engage in the critical communication of culture.

Cultural awareness

> Catholics and pain

The Last Catholic in America (1974) is John R. Powers' (1945-) thinly veiled memoir of life in the late 1950s. Speaking through the young character, Eddie Ryan, he describes a culture that will be familiar to people who went to Catholic schools at that time.

Such people will remember the advice to "offer it up": if a person was suffering from toothache or an accident or some other misfortune, she or he would be advised to "offer it up" for the souls in purgatory or for missionaries or for some other worthy cause.

One could easily have believed that God delighted in human suffering.

While these days children are not often instructed in this way, they still need an outlook that will help them as Christians to cope with life's difficulties.

Cultural awareness

> Nothing is better calculated to win the hearts of people than a resemblance of manners and taste.
> St Ignatius Loyola.

Ignatius Loyola founded the Jesuits. Among his distinguished followers, one of the most brilliant was Matteo Ricci (1552-1610). He was one of those people who are blessed with outstanding ability in many branches of learning.

Eventually finding his way into China, he learned what might be termed classical Chinese, and became a scholar whose works in Chinese earned the respect of established Chinese scholars.

He adopted the dress and customs of these learned people.

In a word, he resembled people in manners and taste and thus won their hearts, as Loyola maintained. In so doing. Ricci faced two dilemmas: how to reconcile elements of a non-Christian culture with Christianity, and how to maintain cordial relations with non-believers.

Teachers have the same kind of balancing act to perform: how to extract and pass on what is good in our culture, and yet communicate with students who are not always disposed to accept Christian ideas.

Cultural awareness

> The publicans, too, came to be baptised: 'Master', they said to [John], 'what are we to do?' He told them, 'Do not go beyond the scale appointed you'. Even the soldiers on guard asked him, 'What of us? What are we to do?' He said to them, 'Do not use people roughly, do not lay false information against them; be content with your pay'.
>
> Luke 3:12-14

We are told that John the Baptist lived in the wilderness, that he wore rough garments, that he ate locusts and wild honey: he was totally other-worldly.

Nevertheless, he found the words to be spot on in explaining what could be expected of the publicans and guards, who inhabited a sub culture on the fringes of, or beyond, respectability.

The respectable were not treated so gently:

> 'You brood of vipers... do not think to say "We have Abraham for our father": I tell you God has power to raise up children of Abraham out of these very stones.'

Teachers need to communicate effectively with the various cultural groups to which our students belong.

Cultural awareness

> There are Parthians among us, and Medes, and Elamites... some of us are visitors from Rome... there are Cretans, too, and Arabians and each has been hearing them [the apostles on Pentecost day] tell of God's wonders in their own language.
>
> Acts 2:9, 11

Perhaps we have travelled overseas and, after battling to make ourselves understood, have experienced the relief of finding someone who can speak our own language. We feel a sense of hope that at last we might be able to solve a pressing problem.

No doubt, many of the foreigners present at the Pentecost event spoke the basic Greek that was used as a common language at that time. Nevertheless, hearing of God's wonders in their own tongue was an obvious bonus for them.

In schools, most mainstream students are able to speak English, even if as a second language. Successful communication about vital matters is not so much about vocabulary as about wavelength: teachers need to show an understanding of the idiom, values, symbols, customs, etc. of their group of students and school.

Each school has its own culture, as indeed, to some extent, does every class. In some cases, teachers will be obeyed but they will not be accepted until they master the cryptic tokens that act as passwords within the students' culture.

Insight is needed to understand the culture of our school, and for the skills to communicate positively.

Cultural awareness

> We stayed some days in [Philippi], and on the Sabbath, we went outside the gate to the bank of the river where we thought there was a place of prayer. Sitting down, we spoke to the women who had gathered there. A certain woman named Lydia, a dealer in purple from the town of Thyatira, who worshipped God, was listening. The Lord opened her heart to give close attention to what Paul was saying. When she and her household were baptised, she urged us, saying, 'Since you have judged me to be a believer in the Lord, come to my home and stay there'. She insisted on our coming.
>
> Acts 16:12-15

When Paul visited Philippi, he set foot on what we now recognise as European soil. Lydia was Paul's first convert there. She dealt in purple dye, a precious commodity. She was obviously a strong woman, one who wouldn't take no for an answer.

Paul chose a setting where he could meet people likely to heed his message. Quite literally, he met them where they were.

He would go on to visit Philippi on two other occasions. He also wrote his converts an epistle, in which he makes it clear how dear these Philippian converts were to him.

Cultural awareness

> As for Jonah, he took it sore amiss, and was an angry man that day. And thus he made his prayer to the Lord: See if this be not the very thought I had far away in my own country!... I knew from the first what manner of God thou art, how kind and merciful, how slow to punish, how rich in pardon, vengeance ever ready to forgo.
>
> Jonah 4:1-2

The reluctant prophet: although summoned by God to go east, overland, Jonah took ship and went west.

The sailors saw him as a jinx and threw him overboard; he was saved by spending three days in the belly of a great sea-beast. Back on task, he went to Nineveh, a city the very mention of which horrified the Jews. Yet, his task was to convert all the Ninevites, from the king down. He achieved incomparable success.

That is why he was so angry: he didn't want to help those he despised.

Some scholars believe that the inspired writer reworked the sources of this charming and colourful story to teach the lesson that we should not despise other cultures, even those of our bitter enemies.

Sadly, we must admit that the lesson is as relevant today as it was when *Jonah* was written. In our country and others, there is often hatred of people who are different.

In trying not to absorb the hostilities in our society, we lead our students to be tolerant.

Cultural awareness

> Aron Jean-Marie Lustiger (1926-2007)

Lustiger was born into the Jewish faith but converted to Catholicism in his youth. During World War II, while most of his family took refuge in the south of France, his mother was sent to Auschwitz, where she died.

He felt called to the priesthood. After serving n various ministries, he was appointed Archbishop of Paris in 1981 and then a Cardinal in 1983. He and other converts have been looked upon as turncoats by some of their former co-religionists, and with suspicion by some Catholics. Such was the lot of Jean-Marie Lustiger.

He wrote the epitaph which is inscribed on his tomb in Notre Dame Cathedral:

> I was born Jewish.
> I received the name of my paternal grandfather, Aaron.
> Having become Christian
> By faith and by baptism
> I have remained Jewish
> As did the Apostles.
> I have as my patron saints
> Aaron, the High Priest,
> Saint John the Apostle,
> Holy Mary, full of grace...

We admire Lustiger. We also admire the many Jews who are, and have been, outstanding artists, writers, thinkers and leaders. We also admire our fellow citizens who just get on with it as Jewish Australians.

We help our students to denounce anti-Semitism.

Cultural awareness

> Chrétien de Chergé (1937-1996)

Chrétien de Chergé was a Cistercian priest, who was Prior of an Abbey in Tibhirne, Algeria.

Before his appointment, he made an extensive study of Islam. He spoke Arabic fluently and built up cordial relationships with the Moslem villagers who lived near his monastery.

Sensing that Islamic fundamentalists were likely to storm the Abbey and murder the priests (which sadly, happened), he wrote to the person who might be his killer:

> ... my last-minute friend, who will not have known what you are doing... I commend you to the God in whose face I see Jesus and may we find each other, happy 'good thieves' in Paradise if it please God, the Father of us both.

Not a passing 'feel-good' gesture but a deep conviction, to the extent of giving up his life for it.

Many people in our society fear Moslems. Some even hate them, possibly without being able to explain why. Our students may absorb hostility. We seek to encourage tolerance.

Cultural awareness

> From the nature of the Catholic school also stems one of the most significant elements of its educational project: the synthesis between culture and faith... All of which demands an atmosphere characterised by the search for truth, in which competent, convinced and coherent educators, teachers of learning and life, may be a reflection, albeit imperfect but still vivid, of the one Teacher.
> *The Catholic School on the Threshold of the Third Millennium*, 1997, paras 14, 15.

The above quotation is taken from a document prepared by the Congregation for Catholic Education.

It is noteworthy first that the synthesis between faith and culture is seen as 'one of the most significant' activities of the school, and second, that 'competent, convinced and coherent' teachers are seen as agents of the integration.

Teachers are seen as searchers after truth, and it is implied that they themselves have managed to make the required synthesis.

The achievement of this synthesis implies that people have reflected upon their culture in the light of faith, embracing what is worthwhile, and rejecting that which is incompatible with Christian life and values.

Cultural awareness

> He then told the guests a parable, noticing how they were choosing the best places at table for themselves ... 'when you are invited, go to the lowest place and recline, so that, when your host enters, he can say to you: "My friend, come up higher". Then you will win distinction from all your fellow guests'.
>
> Luke 14:7, 10, 11

Jesus, noting the way people in his society behaved at a dinner, could here have been quoting from a self-help manual with a title like 'How to get yourself noticed'.

The real point of the parable comes in his words to his host:

'... when you give an entertainment, invite persons that are poor, crippled, blind, lame: and you will be happy, because they have no means of compensating you...'

Fortunately, there have always been Christians who, taking this message literally, have risen to meet its inherent challenges.

For the rest of us, the message is that we should not exclude from life's feast those people who have severe limitations.

In schools these days, there are Special Needs units where special kinds of teachers look after the students.

There are also other students who feel excluded from the mainstream, and again, special kinds of teachers have the gift of reaching out to them.

Our society loves the beautiful people. We seek to be counter-cultural, to open our hearts to all. We esteem those of our colleagues who deal with students who would otherwise feel like outsiders.

Cultural awareness

> Now while Paul was waiting for them at Athens, his soul was exasperated on seeing how the city was wholly given up to idolatry... Then [he] stood up in the midst of the Areopagus, and said, 'Men of Athens, I see that in every aspect, you are remarkably religious. For as I was going about and observing objects of your worship, I found an altar with this inscription: "To the unknown God". What, therefore you worship unknowingly, I make known to you...'
>
> Acts 17:16, 22-23

Paul was speaking in the Areopagus, an assembly at a place we would call 'the Hill of Mars'. The assembly was made up of senior officials who had served the state without incurring a criminal record.

We see here how Paul reflected on the culture, yet used a serviceable feature to communicate with members of the distinguished gathering. Some ridiculed him, others said they would hear more at another time, while some became believers.

Insight is needed to evaluate our culture and use its elements to communicate with our students.

Cultural awareness

> The Dicastery for Culture and Education 'works for the development of people's human values in the context of Christian anthropology contributing to the full realisation of Christian discipleship'.

This description issued by the Holy See relates to the dicastery, or department of the Roman Curia, formed in 2022 by the merger of two former dicasteries: education and culture.

The terminology may be specialised, but it is clear that human values are esteemed and the dicastery exists to ensure that Christian education is consistent with a sound understanding of human nature.

Documents from the former Congregation for Catholic Education were notable for their understanding of life in contemporary schools. No doubt documents from the new dicastery will also repay close study.

Cultural awareness

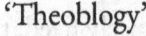
'Theoblogy'

A term coined to describe the study of web logs relating to God: to hazard a guess at the meaning of the term!

The word is a reminder of the pervasiveness of the net, which has become a cultural mainstay. As we all know, you can find practically anything – good or bad – by surfing the net.

We have probably found that it can be a very helpful research tool and a great time waster.

We are familiar with all the warnings about the dangers the net can pose to our students.

There is probably nothing else in our culture which demands a more critical eye, or a greater exercise of everyday self-discipline.

We seek to use technology wisely so that we can lead our students to do the same.

Cultural awareness

> Baby boomers, Generation X, Generation Y (Millennials), Generation Z

These descriptors are not scientifically exact, or used in the same way by everyone, but we can generalise by describing Baby Boomers as those born between 1945 and 1960; Generation X, between 1961 and 1980; Generation Y, between 1981 and 1996, Generation Z, between 1997 and 2010 and Generation Alpha between 2010 and 2024. Those born between 1981 and 1996 are often called Millennials.

If the dates are not precisely fixed, there is even less agreement about the qualities of each generation. For example, some people believe that 'X' was used to indicate that the generation had nothing in particular to distinguish it, and the succeeding generations have just followed alphabetical order. Nevertheless, there are many qualities attributed to each group and they repay reflection.

While Millennials may have much in common with Generation Alpha, older teachers may find it more difficult to bridge the generation gap.

We seek the ability to interpret accurately and compassionately the cultural qualities of groups of teachers and students.

Cultural awareness

> Meanwhile, the elder son was in the field. When he returned and came near the house, he heard strains of music and dancing, and, calling one of the farmhands aside, inquired what all this meant… Thereupon he grew angry and refused to go in. So the father came out and pleaded with him. But he protested and said to the father: 'Look at all these years I have been toiling like a slave for you! … But here comes that son of yours…'
>
> Luke 15:25-26, 28-29, 30

For the elder son, the Prodigal Son is no longer a brother but 'that son of yours'. He realises that his brother has already had his share, and now he is getting another – at the elder brother's expense. A hard lesson of the parable is that the brother must be like his father and forgive, even at great cost to himself.

In contemporary culture, forgiveness and reconciliation are scarcely more popular than they were in the days of Jesus. Movies frequently justify violent retribution, while, in the real world, road rage, brawls and angry confrontations have a certain allure for some people.

People like Nelson Mandela and Desmond Tutu demonstrate the possibility of reconciliation on a grand scale, and we are thankful for their example.

In everyday life, Thomas More may provide us with a useful example. He was not short of people who betrayed him, yet he did not retaliate; he forgave them and as a measure of his forgiveness he prayed that he, and those who hurt him, would, together, eventually be merry in God forever.

Disputes and feuds often occur in schools. Our students need guidance and our example if they are to forgive their brother or sister from the heart (Matthew 18:35), as More did.

Cultural awareness

> ... that brother of yours was dead and has come to life again.
>
> Luke 15:32

The father in the parable had two difficult sons to deal with: one squandered his inheritance and the other was a virtue signaler who sulked.

The compassion the father showed in dealing with his boys is captured in the paintings of James Tissot (1836-1902), copies of which may be seen on the net.

The requisite dispositions are captured in the prayer of the Church:

> Jesus, meek and humble of heart, plant in our hearts your mercy, tolerance, humility and patience towards all people.

These are not exactly the most prized attitudes in our society: to practise them we would be going against the run of play – being counter-cultural.

Cultural awareness

> A false balance the Lord hates: nothing but full weight will content him.
>
> Proverbs 11:1

The Bible contains many references to deceitful scales and weights. The prophet Amos criticised merchants who could not wait for trading to begin so that they could bump up prices and give short measure to their customers.

We know that fraud, particularly at the expense of the most vulnerable, is commonplace and esteemed by people without conscience.

Hopefully, our students will think highly of being fair dinkum and of extending a fair go to all.

Cultural awareness

> ... the shepherds said to one another: 'Let us go over to Bethlehem and find out the truth of this thing the Lord has made known to us'. So they set off in haste and sought out Mary and Joseph and the infant cradled in a manger... At last the shepherds returned, glorifying and praising God for everything they had heard and which afterwards was seen to be just what they were told.
>
> Luke 2:15, 16, 20

The shepherds' life was far from being one of idyllic tranquility. They had to contend with isolation, the weather and danger from wild animals and thieves. They were not always highly thought of. And yet, Luke, in keeping with his theme of the universal reach of the message of salvation, depicts the shepherds as being the first to learn of the birth of their deliverer.

When they found him as a baby in a stable, they recognised the truth that here was a deliverer who was on their level. They rejoiced and praised God who had intervened in this way.

We hope that our students recognise in their school those elements that make its message ring true.

Cultural awareness

> Be lenient towards the offences of others. This is the chief value of courtesy
> Desiderius Erasmus (1566-1536)

Adding to this statement of Erasmus, Hilaire Belloc asserted that courtesy is a manifestation of the grace of God. St Francis de Sales (1567-1622), who did so much to promote holiness of life among ordinary people, wrote "I should like you to cultivate a gentle and sincere courtesy which offends nobody but wins everybody".

In the hurry and bustle of modern life courtesy seems a bit out of date: unless you push and shove you will miss out; it's dog ,eat dog, and make sure you're not bitten last. Push your trolley and everyone else should get out of the way. Grab the remote before anyone else gets to it.

Nobody would encourage some of the more extreme forms of etiquette that were practised in former times, but consideration for others is never out of date, even if some people believe it is unfashionable.

Our school will encourage our students to practise charity through courteous behaviour.

Cultural awareness

> ... the poor [and] the weak... must be helped not with occasional charity but in such a way that they can be raised a little at a time to the standard of life and that level of culture to which they have a right.
> Albino Luciani (later, Pope John Paul I)

The transformation of society, through the protection of the weak and the implementation of the principles of social justice, have always been important to enlightened Christians.

Albino Luciani practised what he preached and encouraged his clergy to do the same. He urged them to sell church treasures and to give the money to the poor. When, as a Bishop, he was transferred from one diocese to another, he remarked that he had gone to the first with five lira in his pocket, and he left with the same amount.

He said that had he not become a priest, he would have become a journalist. He wrote articles to communicate his ideas to the public. His choice of idiom and topics made his articles appealing. Pope John Paul II wrote that his predecessor's skill as a catechist 'amazed us all'.

We would hope that our school, correctly interpreting the ideas that motivate the culture of its families, will communicate successfully with them.

Cultural awareness

> A disconnect

Pope Francis has spoken about a 'disconnect': the gap students may perceive between what a school teaches and the reality of life in their society.

Speaking to students during a visit to Athens, he drew upon Greek myths to make his point.

He recalled that Ulysses had himself bound to the mast so that he could not answer the call of the Sirens.

Orpheus, on the other hand, played melodies superior to those of the Sirens.

The Pope implied that Ulysses stood for schools which do not engage with society and discourage their students from doing so.

The preferable course, in the Pope's opinion, is to imitate Orpheus in a considered engagement.

Cultural awareness

> Stolen water taste sweet and bread eaten in secret is delicious.
> Proverbs 9:17

In the Book of Proverbs, Dame Folly invites all who are simple to come into her abode and follow her attractive but disastrous advice – of which this slogan is an example.

Dame Folly is alive and well in our society.

In our school, we can help our students to see through her specious slogans and make informed choices.

Cultural awareness

A reader used in schools in the eighteenth century was designed to help poor children to find their way in their society, Thus we find instructions about the care of one's wig and how to sit while wearing a sword – guidance not needed nowadays.

Students were also advised to empty their chamber pot immediately on rising, but not to throw the contents out the window or into the street.

We would all agree with the advice about chamber pots, but views will differ about other forms of refuse.

People will debate its nature, source, disposal, economic impact, effects on health...

Schools have the difficult task of framing wise policies and fostering temperate debate.

Cultural awareness

> Life is sweet, brother.
> George Borrow, *Lavengro*. (1851)

George Borrow(1803-1883) was an English writer and traveller. In two novels, *Lavengro* (1851) and *The Romany Rye* (1857), he drew upon the life of the Roma, a race who are more widely known as Gypsies. Found in most countries, yet retaining their own customs, Gypsies are often mistrusted or misunderstood by the wider community.

Ceferino Giménez Malla (1861-1936) was one of the Romani living in Huerca, a northern province in Spain, where the locals speak Catalan.

In a calling not conspicuous for probity, he was a horse trader esteemed for honesty and generosity. He was looked upon as a leader of his own community.

He learned Catalan and fostered good relations between the races.

He was also devoted to his faith, enjoying success as a catechist. It was through this loyalty that he was executed during the Spanish civil war.

In declaring Ceferino Blessed, Pope John Paul noted that he had mediated in 'conflicts that sometimes blur the relations between non-Roma and Roma'.

Some of our students – and colleagues – have to straddle two cultures, with differing customs, values and mindset. It is not always an easy task.

Cultural awareness

AI in the Catholic classroom

The following is the first part of a 500 word reflection on this topic, It was composed by Artificial Intelligence in about thirty seconds.

> Artificial Intelligence (AI) has the potential to revolutionise the Catholic classroom in several ways, but it also raises important ethical questions and challenges that need to be addressed.
>
> One of the most significant benefits of AI in the classroom is its ability to personalise learning experiences for each student. AI-powered systems can analyse student performance data and provide tailored recommendations for further study, helping students to achieve better outcomes. In addition, AI chatbots and virtual assistants can provide students with immediate feedback and support, even outside of class hours. AI can also support teachers by automating repetitive tasks such as grading and administrative duties, allowing them to focus on higher-level tasks such as lesson planning and providing individualised support to students.

It is yet another way in which teachers are called upon to choose what is helpful in AI, and entities like ChatGPT and to perceive their positive uses, while not being blind to abuses.

Cultural awareness

> By the rivers of Babylon, there we sat down, yea, we wept when we remembered Zion.
>
> Psalm 137:1

Between 585 BC and 537 BC, King Nebuchadnezzar of the Chaldeans deported groups of Israelites to Babylon, about 80 kilometres south of modern Baghdad.

The doleful trek would have taken about four months; on arrival in an alien land, they mourned the loss of their homeland and Temple, as the Psalmist records.

The prophet Jeremiah (650 BC-570 BC) had warned his people of impending dangers and had offered strategies to avoid them; unfortunately they were disregarded.

Under divine inspiration, he wrote a letter to the exiles in which he relayed God's instructions to them:

> Build houses and settle down, plant gardens and eat what they produce... Also seek the peace and prosperity of the city to which I have carried you into exile. Pray for it...
>
> Jeremiah 29:5, 7

The families of many of our students and colleagues would have made a similar difficult passage to a new culture. Sadly, for some of them, it may have been a rocky road, and their new environment may not have been welcoming; perhaps it is still not so.

Cultural awareness

> Schools serve the same social functions as prisons and mental institutions to define, control and regulate people.
>
> Michel Foucault

In his *Discipline and Punish* (1975), this French sociologist argued that the disciplinary procedures adopted in Catholic schools for boys in France in the seventeenth and eighteenth centuries were designed to prepare a docile workforce.

The children who attended these schools, first established in 1680, had never before been in a classroom. It took time and skill to train them to cope with instruction in reading, writing, calculations and Religion. The aim was to prepare them to be good Christians and good citizens.

In Australia, Mary MacKillop and her followers also strove to help students from poor families to be good Christians and good citizens. Sister Mary and her Sisters also had their critics.

In today's culture, it is common to denigrate or cancel institutions and individuals who do not measure up to certain people's opinions.

No doubt there are cases that do warrant condemnation, but we strive to help our students not to become unthinking members of the cancel culture.

Cultural awareness

> ... a strong streak of idealism and ample reserves of cynical cunning

This is an appraisal the approach of Konrad Adenauer (1876-1967), first chancellor of the Federal Republic of Germany. He led Germany through reconstruction after World War II and presided over what is termed the 'economic miracle' of Germany's economic resurgence. He steered his country through the competing schemes of the western powers and the Soviet Union and strongly supported European unity.

His idealism was based on his staunch Catholicism; his cunning enabled him to survive Nazism and endless political intrigues. 'Shrewd' would seem to be a fairer description than 'cynical'.

He put into practice the Lord's command to be as cunning as a serpent and as innocent as a dove (Matthew 6:1).

Our students need help to recognise evil for what it is, to unmask wolves in sheep's clothing and yet keep trying to avoid malicious responses. We certainly do not want them to be cynical.

11

On a humane approach: a wise vision of the human condition

> And God said, Let us make man, wearing our own image and likeness: let us put him in command of the fishes of the sea, and all that flies through the air, and the cattle and the whole earth, and all the creeping things that move on earth. So God made man in his own image, made him in the image of God. Man and woman both, he created them... And God saw all that he had made and found it very good.
>
> Genesis 1:26-27, 31
>
> Lord, you give protection to human and beast, so rich is your divine mercy: under the shelter of those wings the frail children of earth will find confidence.
>
> Psalm 35 (36):7
>
> The glory of God is the human being fully alive...
>
> St Irenacus, 130-202
>
> I am a man; I consider nothing human alien to me.
>
> Terence, 170BC
>
> The greatness of humanity is not in being human but in being human
>
> Mahatma Gandhi (1869-1948)

Here, 'humane' includes two of the connotations of the word: esteem for the human, and loving kindness.

Human beings are made in the image of God: he found his creation very good. Further, God the Son embraced human nature, being like us in all things, sin excepted. St Teresa of Avila wrote that 'it is God's will that ... graces should come to us through the hands of Christ in his most holy humanity, that humanity in which his Majesty has proclaimed he is well pleased'.

The Fathers of the Second Vatican Council reminded us that 'the expectation of a new earth must not weaken our anxiety to develop this one; on the contrary it should strengthen it'.

As teachers, we strive to help students to develop as human beings, to contribute to the development of society and to come to the aid of those who live in sub-human conditions.

We pursue this aim by trying to be fine human beings ourselves, and conscious of our shortcomings, by showing to others the same lovingkindness that we hope for ourselves.

A humane approach

> We don't try to convert them. We just do what we can to help them to lead a decent human life.

A group of talented senior students was attending an assembly. A guest speaker had been invited to address them.

They were surprised by his appearance: he wore clothing that seemed to come from an Op Shop. He spoke quietly – in fact he seemed to be exhausted.

When he was introduced as a missionary, the group became restless: they were not noted for sensitivity, compassion or interest in religious topics.

He spoke of the miserable life of the people among whom he lived and worked. It was little better than that of the animals they looked after, with starvation always just around the corner, Whatever the people suffered, he and his co-workers suffered.

His presentation was simple. He did not want anything or ask for anything. He was speaking because a friend who was one of their teachers had invited him.

Here was a human being concerned about other human beings.

In what was for them an unprecedented gesture, the boys spontaneously and generously sent round the hat.

A humane approach

> A basket case

The plight of 42 women who wove baskets in a village near the city of Chittagong in Bangladesh was rendering them a basket case when, in 1976, they came to the attention of Muhammad Yunus, Professor of Economics in the university in that city.

He found that having borrowed at exorbitant rates from loan sharks to buy needed materials, when they made their baskets, they lost whatever profit they made. The women were so poor that no bank would risk making them a loan.

Trusting in their honesty, he lent them money out of his own pocket. They returned his money with a very modest profit.

Formulating the theory of microcredit, he went on to create funds so that poor entrepreneurs could borrow and survive. Eventually, he founded the Grameen (=Village) Bank for this purpose.

In 2006, he was awarded the Nobel Peace Prize in recognition of his efforts. He invested the prize money in causes to further promote human dignity.

A humane approach

> The education of youth, particularly of the poor... assists them to grow in human dignity.
>
> St Joseph Calasanz, Patron of Christian Schools

In Rome, Calasanz and his followers had the daunting experience of introducing the routine of the classroom to students who had never had any experience of school. Members of other congregations would have the same experience in many other countries.

Every founder of the teaching congregations set a high priority on human dignity, not only as a concept, but also through adopting strategies that would help students to live with self-respect as responsible members of society

We ask for a deeper awareness of human dignity and for a continuing enthusiasm to promote it.

A humane approach

> The Holy Father [John Paul II] affirms that 'the need for the Catholic school becomes evidently clear when we consider what it contributes to the development of the mission of the People of God, to the dialogue between Church and the human community, to the safeguarding of freedom of conscience...'
>
> *The Religious Dimension of Education in a Catholic School* (1988), para.34.

The words 'dialogue', 'freedom' and 'conscience' point to three important functions of the Catholic school.

'Dialogue' entails speaking and listening. Unlike 'interrogation', dialogue implies some element of respect for another speaker's opinion and person, some give and take, some quest that goes beyond gathering information.

'Freedom' denotes victory over types of bondage that extend from the physical to the mental, emotional and spiritual.

Persons without conscience are enemies of the human condition; people with a strong social conscience are its friends.

It is a privilege for teachers to help students to develop these attributes.

A humane approach

> Rubbishing other people

Frank Sheed (1897-1981) was born in Australia but it was in the United Kingdom and the United States that he gained respect as a writer, publisher and defender of the Catholic faith.

Reflecting on his days as a member of the Catholic Evidence Guild and as a speaker in London's Hyde Park, where people gathered to hear and debate a wide range of opinions, he realised that if a speaker's aim was to win and put an opponent down, one would inevitably be tempted to cheat.

Unlike many a controversialist, he did not delight in demeaning his opponents: a restraint that requires considerable self-mastery. One has only to read the works of some of the champions of either side in the Reformation to realise how dignified and respectful was Sheed's approach.

The ability to differ from others while treating them with respect is an ornament to any person or society.

We urge our students to treat others with becoming respect.

A humane approach

> In my life, disability has never been seen as a problem or a burden. It is part of my life and an opportunity to do things differently.
>
> Michaela Mycroft (1994-)

Michaela (better known by the diminutive, 'Chaeli') Mycroft was nine months old when it was discovered that she suffers from cerebral palsy. She is a quadriplegic.

In her wheelchair, she has climbed Mt Kilimanjaro and participated in an ultramarathon of 89 kilometres. In this case, she had to fight against regulations that would have prevented her taking part. She is an inspiration.

We are grateful that we live in an age where people with disabilities are not hidden away or exhibited in freak shows.

We salute those teachers who work warmly and so effectively with their disabled students; we admire their students who enjoy significant achievements, those who do the best they can, and we are concerned for those who feel defeated: we recall as Psalm 102, 'A prayer for the lowly when they grow faint'.

A humane approach

> 'Where are they? Has no one condemned you?' She answered, 'No one, sir'. Jesus said, 'Nor do I condemn you. You may go; do not sin again'.
>
> John 8:10-11

If the Gospels generally direct our attention heavenwards, the episode of the woman taken in adultery is very much concerned with the here and now, It is obvious that the woman has been set up. Her supposed lover has betrayed and deserted her. She has been humiliated, publicly shamed and is now threatened with death.

Jesus does not condone what she has done but he refuses to take part in the nonsense that threatened to dehumanise the woman.

Jesus acts like the father of the Prodigal son: without denying the truth of the boy's confession, his first concern was for his son's rehabilitation: 'Quick, bring out the finest robe...'

We may become aware that a colleague is having an affair, or has been wounded by a spouse's affair. Or we may learn that a colleague or a student has had an abortion.

We don't condone what has been done. However, we do not claim to judge. We certainly do not claim the higher moral ground. Rather, we focus, not on the deed, but on helping the person to survive.

A humane approach

> It must never be forgotten that the purpose of instruction at a school is education, that is, the development of persons from within, freeing them from that conditioning which would prevent them from becoming a fully integrated human being. The school must begin from the principle that its educational program is intentionally directed to the growth of the whole person.
>
> *The Catholic School*, para 29.

'The whole person' and 'integral formation' are terms repeatedly used in documents published by the Congregation for Catholic Education.

The development of a person's physical, mental, emotional, spiritual, and moral dimensions is envisaged. Moreover, the development is to be integral: it is hoped that the person will become an integer, a whole human being, characterised by integrity. We recall statements like 'All brawn and no brain'.

These lofty aims require the labour of many hands.

We and our colleagues, sharing these aims, will talk them over together and come up with ways of pursuing them in the context of our own school.

A humane approach

The Dip

(In the following comment, mention is made of Raphael: in the Book of Tobit, the young Tobias is sent on a perilous mission and he is accompanied by the archangel Raphael, who protects and instructs him. Cheshire and his wife Sue Ryder took in and accommodated the ailing and the abandoned, accompanying them like Raphael.)

When Leonard Cheshire visited a place identified as 'the Dip' in Dehradun, Northern India, he saw a drain leading to a refuse dump where there was a group of hovels in which around one hundred people were living.

The hundred or more people were lepers, and the little cluster of huts became the nucleus of Raphael, the first institution opened as a joint venture by Cheshire and Sue Ryder, his wife. To begin with, they housed patients in tents provided by the film director, David Lean, who had been scouting the area in preparation for one of his films. They scrounged other materials, being helped by volunteers who came and are still coming.

Raphael has grown into a centre for treating not only leprosy, but also Tuberculosis, autism and a variety of other illnesses.

Put simply, Raphael exists 'For the relief of suffering without discrimination'.

An equal welcome is extended to Hindus, Moslems, Sikhs and Christians.

A humane approach

> Christian education sees all of humanity as one large family, divided perhaps by historical and political events, but always one in God who is Father of all.
> *The Religious Dimension of Education in a Catholic School*, para. 45

Most schools have students from a variety of ethnic and religious backgrounds. Sometimes, the animosities simmering in their backgrounds boil over in school.

Even when all seems peaceful, we realise that many students harbour real, if unspoken, fears of people of different backgrounds: the prejudices of society are ingrained in them. Most schools have policies to counter discrimination, but many students pay them only lip service.

Merely putting people in the same room or school will not unite them.

Class discussions often uncover antipathies. We understand that to cast lightning bolts of anger or ridicule is to worsen the situation. Example, and patient, consistent exchanges of opinions are called for.

A humane approach

> This above all to thine own self be true...
> *Hamlet* I, iii, 78

Although he lacked the wisdom to guide his own conduct, Polonius had the gift of expressing truths succinctly.

One cannot argue with the importance of a true sense of selfhood.

Some students need help in moderating their budding delusions of grandeur. Others need help to shed their destructive self-image. Sadly, others need help to overcome the effects of poisonous experiences. In fact, all of us need help to arrive at a true sense of self, a process which remains a work in progress.

Always, we need to be treated with understanding, and always, with lovingkindness.

We remember gratefully those who have intervened lovingly in forming our sense of selfhood, and work to offer the same benefit to the students confided to our care.

Reflections

A humane approach

> Christian education must promote respect for the State and its representatives, the observance of just laws, and a search for the common good. Therefore, traditional civic values such as freedom, justice, the nobility of work and the need to pursue social progress are all included among the school goals, and the life of the school gives witness to them. The national anniversaries and other important civic events are commemorated and celebrated in appropriate ways in the schools of each country.
> *The Religious Dimension of Education in a Catholic School*, para. 45.

An Australian author wrote that to love the little platoon we belong to in society is the seed of public welfare.

As students develop, the group they belong to extends beyond the class, to the school, to new environments... in some cases to the wider community: much depends upon a person's gifts and vision.

We would hope that students are inspired by their life at school to be (as Fr Pedro Arrupe SJ put it) people for others, committed to service for the common good of humanity.

A humane approach

> In conclusion, brothers and sisters, whatever is true, whatever is honourable, whatever just, whatever pure, whatever lovable, whatever merits praise – if there be any virtue, if anything worthy of praise – such are the things that you should keep in mind.
>
> Philippians 4:8

These words inspired the architect of a very influential program in a government school.

He wanted to frame courses that would sample the best of human achievements and engage the students.

He was fortunate in piloting the program in a small school, where all members of staff shared his vision, and all participated in planning.

We help our students to keep in mind whatever is true, honourable, just, lovable, and praiseworthy.

A humane approach

When John died in his early fifties, former students from all over Australia came to his funeral.

He was the essential humane teacher.

It was obvious to his students that he took his work seriously: his work was well prepared; his delivery was clear; his feedback was punctually and constructively completed; his disposition was consistently pleasant – he was a true professional.

He furthered his studies part time; his love for his subject enthused many students to follow his example.

At a time when students were addressed by their surname, he used Christian names, not as a ploy, but as an expression of the interest he had in each. His students felt that he understood them, that he liked them.

He promoted high ideals, but he had a realistic understanding of the human condition, accepting students' shortcomings – and his own – with good humour.

He valued the human and the divine. His students still cherish his vision.

A humane approach

> Inoffensive people

In Franz Kafka's novel, *The Trial*, one day the inoffensive Joseph K. finds himself, out of the blue, betrayed and arrested.

We are familiar with stories of brave women and men who single-handedly triumphed over the forces and scoundrels ranged against them.

Franz Kafka (died 1924), on the other hand, excelled at exploring the nightmarish experiences of 'insignificant' people who, for reasons they cannot understand, are crushed by powerful forces and officials.

It is difficult to strike a balance between the rights of the individual and those of their group. There is a great temptation to side with the strong against the weak, to sacrifice the voiceless to silence the nagging of the powerful.

In schools, as in other institutions, pressure groups can develop; they clamour to have their ideas implemented.

In schools, just as much as in society at large, some persons may be deemed expendable to appease the pressure groups.

As Christians, we are called to recognise the innate dignity and worth of each individual.

We trust that the treatment our students – and colleagues and families – receive at our school will foster a belief in the importance of each individual and an unwillingness to classify anyone as insignificant.

A humane approach

> ... the two disciples followed Jesus. Jesus turned round and, seeing them follow said to them: 'What is your wish?' They replied: 'Rabbi... where are you staying?' 'Come and you will see', he said to them. So they went and saw where he was staying. They were his guests that day.
>
> John 1:38-39.

We read of occasions when Jesus was a guest. This time he was the host. Commentators say that those who, like Jesus and two of John's disciples, came to John the Baptist, they stayed temporarily in makeshift shelters of branches.

Elsewhere, we hear that in Capharnaum 'news spread that he was at home'. We are not told what happened there. Nor do we learn how Jesus entertained his guests.

At the Last Supper, Jesus was the host in every sense of the word, celebrating with his disciples in keeping with their culture.

Hospitality has been a keynote of Christian communities since the beginning, whether in the context of Eucharistic meals or merely the welcoming of guests or strangers.

Hospitality can inspire hosts to put guests' needs before their own, and guests to accept kindness graciously. Entertaining others can lead to heart-warming human exchanges. To be honest, of course, some social occasions can be very tense, calling upon all our reserves of charity, patience and tact.

There are numerous occasions when schools play host; many schools include students in the routine of welcoming and entertaining guests. Sometimes, the prospect of the visitors' mission can be daunting, but they must be welcomed just the same.

We seek the generosity of spirit to include all guests in our fellowship.

A humane approach

> Tyranny is always better organised than freedom.
> Charles Peguy (1873-1914)

While Peguy, an idealist who abandoned Christianity only later to rediscover it enthusiastically, wrote works of great length, he is best known these days for short statements like the above.

There can be no doubt that the forces which can dehumanise people are well organised. We can cite the competence of those who manufacture, distribute and sell drugs, some of which are described as 'recreational',

Drugs are an extreme example. Violence, intimidation, fear, poverty: these and other evils succeed because those responsible for them are powerful.

There are insidious agents as well, with slogans and images endlessly brought to our attention. How many girls and boys feel inferior because they do not measure up to stereotypes constantly represented to them! Indeed, how many of us adults suffer from feelings of inadequacy because we do not measure up to standards it has pleased some guru to invent.

We are called upon to help our children to escape from the conditioning which can dehumanise them.

A humane approach

> If decade after decade the truth cannot be told,
> each person's mind begins to roam irretrievably.
> Alexander Solzhenitsyn, *Cancer Ward*.

Solzhenitsyn (1918-2008) spent a lifetime campaigning for, and suffering for, the truth: the truth about the Soviet Gulags, and the truth about decadence in the West.

At great personal cost, he maintained the view that without reverence for truth, societies lose their bearings.

We come to realise that the pursuit of illusions and delusions leads not to happiness but to disenchantment.

At a certain school, the tradition has grown up that, regardless of the seriousness of a misdemeanour, even of illegal behaviour, students refuse to lie to protect themselves. How this love for truth developed is a mystery, but it is something to be treasured.

A humane approach

> God of compassion, may we be full of kind actions today; may everyone experience our humanity.
> Roman Breviary

As the petition implies, kindness is inspired by the recognition both of God's compassion and human solidarity.

St Paul tells us that love is patient and kind.

Our own experience has shown us the lift that acts of kindness can confer. They can make the miserable feel more human.

We might find the petition helpful.

A humane approach

> 'Brother Wolf, you have done many evil things in this neighbourhood...'

According to legend, when St Francis was in Gubbio in 1220, he found the inhabitants terrified by a savage wolf.

Francis addressed the wolf, extracting a promise that in return for food he would no longer attack people or other animals. The wolf showed his agreement by putting his paw in Francis' hand.

Many people imitate St Francis in treating animals as fellow creatures loved by God.

Others support the work of the Society for the Prevention of Cruelty to Animals which was founded in England in 1824, and has since spread to many other countries.

Children love their pets. Society shows its strong disapproval of cruelty to animals.

There are many ways in which students can be helped to support the humane treatment of animals.

12

On balance: 'sanctified common sense'

> ... in whatever circumstances I am, I have learned to be content. I know how to live in privation, and I know how to live in abundance. I have been initiated into each and every condition: of satiety and hunger, of abundance and of want. I can do all things in him who strengthens me.
>
> Philippians 4:11-13

All people have to deal with good times and bad, and with conflicting demands. We all seek to strike a balance and to achieve the contentment of which St Paul wrote.

The balance we strike becomes part of ourselves. As teachers, our balance or imbalance is constantly on display, influencing our students for good or ill.

Balance

> '...too, too, sick-making...'
> Miss Agatha Runcible in Evelyn Waugh's *Vile Bodies*.

Evelyn Waugh (1903-1966) may be recalled as the author of *Brideshead Revisited*, adapted as a successful TV series and movie.

Miss Agatha Runcible is a character in his earlier work, Vile Bodies, in which he lampooned the unbalanced behaviour of the in-crowd.

Here. in her characteristic way. she is lamenting some quite reasonable restriction on her outlandish plans.

Balance

> Befriend yourself doing God's will with endurance... and banish your sad thoughts: sadness has been the death of many; no good will come of it.
> Sirach 30:24-25

Jesus commands us to love our neighbour as ourselves, the premise being that we do in fact love ourselves.

We sometimes hear people criticised in terms like 'He/she loves himself/herself'. No doubt there are people who are besotted with themselves.

The chances are that most of us find things about ourselves we do not like. We may become dejected at our lack of success in overcoming them.

As the inspired writer tells us, no good comes from sadness that feeds on itself.

On balance: 'sanctified common sense'

Balance

When Jesus' disciples returned, rejoicing from a training mission, he was elated and offered up prayers of thanksgiving.

At the end, his visible supporters were a few women and one man. He was an object of scorn; he felt forsaken.

In between these times, he was surprised, disappointed and he wept.

If such ups and downs characterised his life and ministry, those whom he has invited to work with him can scarcely expect anything different. As he remarked to the women who mourned his fate: 'If they do this to the wood that is green, what will happen to the wood that is dry?'

We pray for the grace to accept the good times with gratitude and the hard times with faith and courage.

Balance

> Do not be entangled, my child, in too many enterprises. The rich person pays forfeit chasing what overtake they may not, or fleeing what they may not shun. Some people's lives are all toil and haste and anxiety, yet the more they toil, the less advantage they win, through lack of piety.
>
> Sirach 11:10-11

It is easy to get bogged down in class work, extracurricular activities, meetings, professional associations, part-time study, administrative duties, social functions, fund raising projects, buildings, maintenance...

All of these can contribute to the common good, but one person cannot do justice to all of them.

Sometimes, such concerns can eat away at time and energy that should be devoted to those with whom we live.

Jesus told Martha that she was fretful about too many things.

We might pray for the wisdom to understand what is genuinely demanded of us and for the strength to give up the pursuits that cause harm to those with whom we live – and, of course, to ourselves.

Balance

> Three sights warm my heart – God and humans wish them well: peace in the clan, goodwill among neighbours, husband and wife well matched.
>
> Sirach 25:1.

May such good fortune be ours.

Balance

> Christ... continually fulfils his prophetic office... not only through the hierarchy... but also through the laity, whom he made his witness and to whom he gives understanding of the faith and an attractiveness of speech, so that the power of the Gospel might shine forth in their daily social and family life.
>
> Vatican II, *Lumen Gentium*.

Our faith should cheer our life at work and with our family and friends.

St Thomas More is a wonderful model in this matter. He was Lord Chancellor of England; he was also a loving family man, a sought-after guest and host. He was noted for his wit; to amuse his guests, he employed a Fool, or entertainer; he kept a good table; he mixed with what we might term the movers and shakers of his time – all this without sacrificing his principles: everyone knew what he stood for.

Balance

> That they may be one, that they may be one.

As he lay dying, Pope John XXIII prayed for unity, particularly among Christian churches.

As he had lived, so he died.

At our school, it is very likely that there are students and staff who belong to other Christian churches. Frequently they are outstanding in their Christian witness and in their support for the work of the school.

Theologians and Church leaders have the responsibility to explore and clarify doctrinal and administrative matters relating to Church unity.

We who daily work with people of other faiths can thank God for their witness and pray with them.

In the past, there have been tragic divisions and excesses accompanied by bitterness and bigotry. We can be certain that God does not will these unbalanced attitudes.

Balance

> The cobblers' children have no shoes.

A variant to this old saying is that 'The cobbler's children are the worst shod'.

In whichever form, the saying is a reminder that the family of any kind of breadwinner may miss out on the benefits of his or her profession or occupation.

There is always the danger that, having spent the day dealing with other peoples' children, we have no energy left to deal with our own. Or, insisting that our children match the attainment of one of our star pupils, we may exert pressure on them that we would not exert on others' children.

Perhaps one of our children may spectacularly break a school rule or the law. We may be torn between concern for our own tarnished image and the welfare of our child. We hope for wisdom and compassion in such circumstances.

Balance

> From thinking that great courts immure
> All, or no happiness, or that this earth
>   Is only for our prison framed
>   Or that thou art covetous
> To them that thou lov'st, or that they are maimed
> From reaching this world's sweet who seek thee thus
> With all their might, good Lord deliver us.
>
> John Donne, 'Good Lord deliver us'

There have always been people who believe that the things of this world are to be despised by those who seek to love God, or that the world is a prison where we are detained and punished until we go to heaven.

We all know that there is much in society that should be condemned, but there is also so much that is good.

The Anglican poet and priest, John Donne, prayed for a balanced understanding of the human condition.

Our students need help not to see sin everywhere and not to see it anywhere.

We might pray for the wisdom to appraise human institutions in a balanced way and for the ability to share this outlook with our students.

Balance

> ... for my state of life, be neither poverty mine nor riches. Grant me only the livelihood I need: so shall not abundance tempt me to disown you and doubt if Lord there be, nor want bid me steal, and dishonour my Lord's name with perjury.
>
> Proverbs 30:8-9

It's easy to ask not to be poor, but it's a tough call to pray not to be rich.

There are few of us who can honestly sing the Gershwin song 'I've got plenty of nothing and nothing is plenty for me'.

But, on the other hand, we all deplore the behaviour and attitudes of Ebenezer Scrooge whose hoarded wealth made him miserable.

We hope to strike a balance.

Balance

People who have seen Peter Shaffer's play *Amadeus* or the film based on the play will be familiar with the representation of the composer Antonio Salieri as the murderer of Mozart.

According to this representation and to an associated (but contested) tradition that goes back to the time of Salieri's death, the motive was jealousy.

In *Amadeus*, the dying Salieri, conscious of Mozart's genius, declares himself to be the patron saint of mediocrity.

Nobody would care to invoke such a saint; no one would care to be described as mediocre. We may be people of modest talents, but we would not wish to be mediocre.

We interpret mediocrity as selling out, settling for what is comfortable, going through the motions, being lukewarm

This kind of equilibrium is a sad form of compromise.

Balance

> Well had the boding tremblers learned to trace
> The day's disaster in his morning face.

Oliver Goldsmith's Village Schoolmaster was evidently a person of varying moods, which he took out on his pupils. They had learned to recognise what his mood would be on any particular day.

While we differ in our susceptibility to moods, we would all agree that it is unfair to make students suffer for them.

In a profession that involves so much interaction with others, it is obviously advisable to strive for an even disposition and to leave our personal troubles at the classroom door.

We keep working to acquire an even disposition and regret the times that we have let our feelings determine how we treat our students.

Balance

> Sanctified common sense
>
> — Mother Esther

Emma Silcock (1858-1931) joined an Anglican order of Sisters in England. Following a back injury, she was sent to Australia to recuperate.

She became involved in charitable activities in Melbourne and was joined by like-minded women who eventually became the Community of the Holy Name. The Sisters established Refuges, dispensaries, schools and various other foundations to relieve misery.

Now known as Mother Esther, this foundress was an intrepid and astute administrator.

She was shrewd judge of character, demanding a balanced outlook of her followers: together with their spiritual life, they were to have their feet firmly on the ground, practising 'sanctified common sense'.

Some people maintain that nothing is so uncommon as common sense.

We might pray to share Mother Esther's balanced outlook.

Balance

> Therefore a sabbath rest still awaits the people of God...
>
> — Hebrews 4:10

Pope Francis has spoken in favour of a day of rest.

In a *Sixty Minutes* interview in 2018, he was commenting on the Jewish practice of Sabbath rest: 'One day of the week. That's the least! Out of gratitude, to worship God, to spend time with the family, to play, to do all these things. We are not machines'.

Earlier (2014), in his encyclical *Laudato Si'*, he wrote 'Rest opens our eyes to the larger picture and gives us renewed sensitivity to the rights of others'.

Teachers' lives are intensely active and there is always the danger that they will be consumed by a myriad of concerns.

Regular rest can provide some balance.

And then there is the possibility, suggested by Pope Francis, that our rest can have a spiritual dimension.

Balance

> Middle of the road; middle of the roader; middle of the roadism

The term, 'middle of the road', political in origin and coined in the late nineteenth century, denotes avoidance of extremes.

The statement 'Virtues lies in the middle course' is of much earlier origin. Thomas Aquinas formulated it, inspired by the Greek philosopher, Aristotle.

Terms like 'even tempered' are based on this principle, as opposed to 'over the top', and 'don't get carried away'.

Moderate behaviour becomes a teacher.

Balance

> ... the restless panting of their being.

In John Henry Newman's 1865 poem, *The Dream of Gerontius*, a dying man is assailed by spirits whose very essence is restlessness.

We have all been plagued by students who cannot sit still.

We have had to deal with colleagues who are always apprehensive, always dreading disasters that might, or might not occur, always perceiving some slight, always suspicious of others' motives, always abandoning a half-finished task to get on with the next, always checking their mobile lest they fail to make an immediate response, always grizzling, always commenting, always finding fault, always offering advice...

We hope not to be of their number.

Balance

> *Balance: A Story of Faith, Family and Life on the Line*

This is the title of a memoir by Nik Wallenda (1979-) who has walked on a high wire above the Niagara Falls and a section of the Grand Canyon, to name just a few of his achievements.

He prepares for his walks with meticulous planning, extensive physical training-and a habit of frequent prayer.

The result is a skilled performance, which may include humorous interludes like lying or sitting on the wire or making a phone call.

We all wish we had his prayerful cool headedness when we have to do a balancing act between colleagues or factions or principles.

Balance

> Take care not to practise your religion before others just to catch their eyes.
>
> Matthew 6:1

People who make a show of conforming to popular causes, or uttering politically-correct statements are sometimes called 'virtue signallers'.

They scorn those who do not agree with them

It is difficult for adults to discern truth from falsehood and to avoid being disturbed by virtue signallers.

How much harder for our students!

Balance

> We need all this to make life livable.
> St Teresa of Avila (1515-1582)

Teresa was a Nun, a cook, a gardener, a reformer, an administrator, a mystic, a writer, a saint and a Doctor of the Church.

She was also known to sing and dance, to play the drum and pipes as well as composing songs. On one occasion, when reprimanded by a person who considered herself an authority on the way Nuns should behave in community, Sister Teresa replied that 'We need all this to make life livable'.

It's likely that sometimes we will come across arrangements which, while not being perfect, nevertheless help colleagues or students to survive. It's then appropriate to recall the saying attributed to Bert Lance, an adviser to President Jimmy Carter: 'If it ain't broke, don't fix it'.

13

On weighing it all up: achievements

Teaching will not make us rich. It won't make most of us famous.

We would hope that it brings us a sense of achievement and fulfilment and that it will make a difference to our students and to the community.

In a wider context, we would hope that it brings us closer to God, and eventually to heaven.

Weighing it all up

> Epitaphs

Arthur Koestler (1905-1983) suggested that his epitaph might state that, despite his best efforts, his achievements were not good enough.

He was born into a Jewish family in Hungary. His life experiences led him to be fluent in Hungarian, German, French, Hebrew and English. He wrote for publication in all of these languages and later in life wrote only in English. Perhaps, we may recall reading his *Darkness at Noon* at school.

He joined the Communist party and then resigned in protest at the behaviour of Joseph Stalin.

He became involved in many causes.

His was a full life, with many successes, but like us all he recognised his limitations.

Weighing it all up

> All will be learners in God's own school.
> John 6:45

The above rendering of Isaiah 54:13 in John's Gospel reminds us that the Lord is continually giving us the chance to learn

We are conscious of spending our lives as teachers. It is perhaps too easy to forget that we are also always students.

If only we are attentive, we can realise that God uses our work, our relationships and the events of our lives to teach us that he loves us, and how to love him.

And this truth applies to others as well: we all have the opportunity to learn from God and each other.

Weighing it all up

> Why not be a teacher?

In a scene in Robert Bolt's *A Man for all Seasons*, Thomas More is seen parrying the attempts of the up and coming Richard Rich to gain entry a to career at court. Sensing the weakness in Rich's character, More declines, suggesting teaching as an alternative - one that would please the court of Heaven. Evidently not Rich's prime concern.

More was right about Rich: it was Rich who eventually perjured himself at More's trial. Thus, More was found guilty of high treason and condemned to death.

The conversation may not have taken place, but we hope that our work in the classroom has won the approval of the court of Heaven.

Weighing it all up

> ... but the Lord's mercies have never failed me: what return shall I make to him?
>
> Psalm 115:3

St Ignatius Loyola, that noted spiritual guide, suggests that one of the ways in which we may dispose ourselves to be conscious of the love of God is to recall the many blessings we have received and to be filled with gratitude for them.

Here we might consider our profession and some of the many blessings we have received in relation to it.

We will have had the enduring affection and support of mentors.

We will have been blessed with the friendship and support of many wonderful colleagues.

We will have had the privilege of working with numerous students who have given us joy.

We will have contributed to the project of making children numerate and literate.

We will have introduced children to the storehouse of human wisdom.

We will have introduced them to the wonders of science and the arts.

We have had the privilege of making them aware of the treasure house of human wisdom.

We have shared in helping them to develop a balanced understanding or their faith

In our ministry, we have striven by word and example to bring them closer to Christ.

We may have been rewarded by seeing some of them do well.

We may have witnessed their commitment to social justice.

We thank God for the vocation of being a teacher, and for the graces he has showered upon us.

Weighing it all up

> ... if one of you strays from the truth and is brought back by another, know that whoever brings back a sinner from wandering will mean saving the sinner's soul from death and throwing a veil over a multitude of sins.
>
> James 5:19-20

It is probable that, in the course of our teaching career, we will have helped students to get back onto the right path.

We may well be ignorant of the fact. Some kind word or deed may have borne fruit long after the occasion we were responsible for them.

In performing this office, we will have been imitating the Good Shepherd who went out of his way to find the strays.

We might pray, thanking God for allowing us to work with him. We might also pray for those of our students who have strayed.

Weighing it all up

> Bright shall be the glory of wise counsellors, as the radiance of the sky above; starry-bright forever their glory who have taught many the right way.
>
> Daniel 12:3

We have all heard of the ripple effect: when a stone is thrown into a pond, the ripples go out into ever-widening circles.

No doubt, we have been wise counsellors to many students and we will have taught the right way to many more.

The impact of our influence – of our words and deeds – may affect the students' families, friends and society at large: all of these things are in the hands of Providence.

We thank God for any good we may have done.

Weighing it all up

We realise that we have not always been successful; indeed it is possible that we have alienated some of our students.

A prayer from the Roman breviary may be helpful:

Look upon those who have fallen away
because of our ill-intent.
Help them and teach us
so that justice and charity may eventually prevail.

Weighing it all up

> Come, you that have received a blessing from my Father, take possession of the kingdom that has been prepared for you since the foundation of the world. For I was hungry and you gave me food... Whereupon the just will answer, 'Lord, when was it that we saw you hungry...' and the King will answer them, 'Believe me, when you did it to one of the least of the members of my family here, you did it to me'.
>
> Matthew 25:34, 35, 37, 40

Faith tells us that in dealing with others – parents, colleagues, children – we are dealing with Christ himself.

We acknowledge that our service has not been perfect, but it has been directly associated with the proclamation of the Kingdom.

We trust in God's mercy, and hope that we will receive the reward that Jesus promised to those who serve him in others.

Some prayers for teachers

Prayer of the Teacher before School

Composed by a Frenchman, Father Rollin (died 1743), it has been in constant use since. The following is an adaptation.

O Lord, you are the source and mainstay of my patience, strength, light
and sound judgment.
It is you who will enable me to touch the hearts of the children confided to my care.
Please don't leave me to my own devices.
Teach me to be humane.
Help me to be a true and trustworthy colleague.
Fill my students and me with the spirit of your Son, Jesus
– I unite all my work with his.
I ask Mary, the mother and teacher of Jesus,
and all those saintly teachers who now rejoice with you,
to pray for me as I go about the work
you have given me.
Amen.

Teacher's Prayer

Source unknown

I want to teach my students how to live this life on earth To face its struggles and its strife and improve their worth Not just the lesson in a book or how the rivers flow But how to choose the proper path wherever they may go To understand eternal truth and know the right from wrong And gather all the beauty of a flower and a song For if I help the world to grow in wisdom and in grace I shall feel that I have won and I have filled my place And so I ask your guidance, God, that I may do my part For character and confidence and happiness of heart.

A Prayer

Composed by Dr Samuel Johnson (1709-1784)

Almighty God, our heavenly Father, without whose help labour is useless, without whose light search is vain, invigorate my studies and direct my enquiries, that I may with due diligence and right discernment establish myself and others in thy holy Faith. Take not, O Lord, thy Holy Spirit from me, let not evil thoughts have dominion of my mind. Let me not linger in ignorance and doubt, but enlighten and support me for the sake of Jesus Christ our Lord. Amen.

A prayer

Author unknown

Lord God You gave saintly teachers to the Church to show the way of salvation to their people, grant that, inspired by their example, we may so follow Christ our Master that together with our students and colleagues we may come at length into your presence. We make this prayer through Christ our Lord, Amen.

www.ingramcontent.com/pod-product-compliance
Lightning Source LLC
Chambersburg PA
CBHW012004090526
44590CB00026B/3863